A Practical Guide for
Outwitting Today's Con Artist
FOR THE 50+ GENERATION

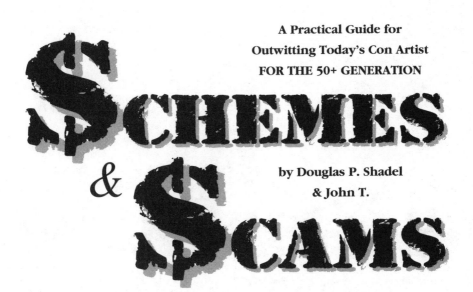

$CHEMES & $CAMS

by Douglas P. Shadel
& John T.

Foreword by
WALTER CRONKITE

Mature Media
1994 SM
NATIONAL AWARDS
WINNER

Newcastle Publishing
North Hollywood, California

SEAFIRST BANK

MEMBER FDIC

Serving Washington for 125 years.

This book is not intended in any way to act as a replacement for legal consultation when needed. The authors and publisher of this book do not guarantee the efficacy of any of the methods herein described, and strongly suggest that at the first suspicion of any illegal activity the reader consult the appropriate legal and/or law enforcement agencies.

Edited by Gina Misiroglu
Cover and interior design by Michele Lanci-Altomare

ISBN: 0-87877-186-7
10 9 8 7 6 5 4 3

PREFACE

I have often heard it said that experience is the best teacher. However, according to Vernon Law, "Experience is a hard teacher because she gives the test first and the lesson afterwards." Sadly, for many people the test is very painful, and often devastating. On the positive side, however, it is fair to say that while we can learn a lot from experience, it need not be limited to our own experience. We can definitely learn from the experience of others.

In the pages that follow, we all have the opportunity to benefit from the experiences of the authors of this book. We have before us the experiences of someone who has worked as a fraud investigator for over thirteen years. In addition, we have the benefit of the experience of a man who worked successfully as a con artist. Perhaps, most of all, we have the experiences of the many people whose encounters with schemes and scams provide some very interesting and instructive reading.

One of the most helpful aspects of this book is that it opens our eyes to the variety of creative ways in which unscrupulous people can and will take advantage of us. My guess is that all of us have been or will be exposed to one of the scams described in this book. Fortunately, we do not have to rely on our own experience to learn about them.

These warnings are especially important to people as they get older. As the authors point out, with only 12 percent of the population, people sixty-five and older account for 30 percent of all fraud victims. The most effective and, hence, most dangerous scams are connected to basic needs: health and financial security. Since we are all interested in something that might improve the quality of our lives in these areas we become vulnerable to those who gain our confidence. It is easy to understand why these scams are often referred to as confidence or "con" games.

In the area of consumer fraud, it is absolutely true that forewarned is forearmed. Both Doug Shadel and John T. make it very clear to us that while regulation, better law enforcement, and imprisonment all play a role, the most effective means by which we can prevent ourselves from becoming the victims of such fraud is to have the kind of information and guidance provided in these pages.

I have a couple of suggestions for anyone who wants to avoid becoming a victim of fraud. First, read this book carefully. Second, post the top ten fraud prevention tips from page 70 next to every telephone in your house.

Finally, our own experience should have taught us that there are few, if any, unearned rewards. Whenever you are offered something "too good to be true," be on guard!

— Horace B. Deets, Executive Director AARP

ACKNOWLEDGMENTS

The following people have been instrumental to the successful completion of this book. I would like to thank: Ken Eikenberry for his long-standing support and willingness to let me experiment and innovate, a rare quality among modern public officials; Gina Misiroglu for her focused editorial advice and comments; the late Bill "B. J." Johnston, for teaching me his editorial writing class during camping trips to British Columbia; Nicholas Shadel for his patience and positive outlook as I spent countless hours writing; Karen Reyes for her support of the project and editorial advice early on; Al Saunders for his sage wisdom and calm demeanor throughout the editing and production processes; Bill Shadel for encouraging me to finish the book and for teaching me how to write while fly fishing on the Dean River; John T. for the willingness to tell his story and for the courage to turn a negative life experience into a national prevention campaign that has helped millions of people lead better lives.

Finally, I would like to thank the members of my own "Fraud Fighter Hall of Fame": lawyers, investigators, and reporters whose dedication and relentless commitment to protecting consumers over the years has been an inspiration to me: Karl Boettner, the late Janet Bridgman, Andy Carter, Jon Ferguson, Betsy Hollingsworth, the late Cal Leach, Lee Norrgard, Renee Olbricht, Susan Patrick, Larry Shannon, Katie Sloan, Robin Talbert, Rick Thomas, Doug Walsh, P. J. Ward, and Herb Weisbaum.

These folks over the years have been the most effective consumer advocates in the United States. I have often thought that if all of these players were put on a single team to fight fraud, there is no limit to what they could do. Thank you all.

TABLE OF CONTENTS

FOREWORD

There is a strange paradox about us human beings—a paradox that can cost us dearly.

The paradox is as complicated as the makeup of our character. On the one hand, most of us are born with or learn (I'll leave *that* one to the geneticists) a set of values that includes a certain trust of our fellow man. We couldn't function very well without that confidence that our neighbor is at least nearly as kindly, unselfish, and trustworthy as we are. We consider it highly aberrational if he does not live within what we consider to be the norms of our society.

The other side of the paradox is that we place that trust in the hands of others who we do not know *for the purpose of material gain*—in other words, to feed our own selfish interests.

A not infrequent result of that conflict of ideals and purposes is that we are severely punished. We get stung. Those in whom we put our trust turn out to be unworthy of it—even, as perhaps we have been unworthy of ourselves in seeking something for nothing.

Of course, the punishment in these cases hardly fits the crime. To profit by a good investment is not only sensible but is the incentive which is at the very base of our free market, capitalistic system—a system that has served us well. We don't deserve to be deceived at great expense when simply trying to enjoy its benefits.

The swindler's crime, on the other hand, is one of the basest of anti-social transgressions. His prey is, indeed, the most innocent and naive among us, and frequently the most vulnerable—the old and dependent whose resources, in both cash and information to protect it, are limited.

Human nature being what it is—both among the trustworthy and those who would exploit them—we undoubtedly always will have, as civilization always has had, the scalawags and their victims. But volumes like this should help illuminate the dark byways of the crooks and alert the rest of us against wandering into their traps.

—**Walter Cronkite**

INTRODUCTION

"George, we have this amazing new computer program that can actually predict movement in the price of gold and silver on a daily basis. But I don't expect you to believe me . . . and you shouldn't either because there are a lot of scams going on out there. So I want to prove myself to you. Now today the price of silver is at 7. According to my projections, the price will go up by next week. You write that down and put it by your phone because I'm going to call you next week and you can tell me if I was right or not."

—John T., 1985

Would you fall for this pitch? It sounds foolproof doesn't it? Here is an investment broker telling you that there are plenty of scams out there and he is going to prove to you that he can make you money by predicting movement in the price of silver before asking you to invest.

What he doesn't tell you is that he has told the same thing to one hundred potential investors, that is, almost the same thing. He tells fifty of them that the price of silver is going to go down and fifty of them that the price is going to go up. Unless the price of silver remains exactly the same, he has fifty people he can call the following week and say, "Well, how did we do?"

This book is based upon over thirteen years of work I have done as a fraud investigator and later as a special assistant to the Washington State attorney general.

For the first six years, I ran a street-front consumer protection office for the attorney general. This gave me the opportunity to see and investigate just about every kind of scheme there was in the marketplace.

Further, because the office was located in Olympia, the state capitol, fraud investigators and prosecutors from all over the country would call my office to discuss various con artists and fraudulent operations that were working throughout the fifty states.

While running the attorney general's consumer protection division, I also became involved with the local senior center, joining their board of directors in 1980. My interest in senior issues was motivated by the realization early on that many of the victims in cases we prosecuted were older adults.

One of the first things we tried to do as early as 1980 was give speeches to folks at the local senior center explaining how scams worked so they could protect themselves. One of the more popular parts of these presentations was the reenactments of fraud schemes. I had written skits which enabled amateur actors (like me) to act out how the bank examiner hoax actually worked.

As hokey as they were, audiences got a big kick out of them and, more importantly, the format seemed to hold their attention better than someone standing up in front of a group and just talking. The popularity of those early presentations using skits explains, in part, why the material in this book is presented the way it is.

The television generation of the 1990s would rather see events occurring in the first person rather than described narratively. They want to be part of the action. Thus most of the scams are presented as pitches: what you would actually hear when confronted by a con artist.

While I have always been interested in prevention, in conjunction with aggressive prosecution, over time I became frustrated with the futility of our efforts to catch con artists.

Of the hundreds of cases I worked on in the 1980s, I can count on one hand the number of times we were successful in getting a consumer's money back for him or her.

The straw that broke the camel's back was a case I worked on in the mid-1980s involving a company called Desert Investments. This company had taken over $3.5 million from five hundred older adults in the Vancouver, Washington, area by selling phony real estate investments. I spent 2,400 hours on this case, virtually living in a hotel room in Vancouver for a year.

When we finally drove the company into bankruptcy, most of the money had been skimmed and investors lost 90 percent of their capital. For many of the victims, the money they invested with Desert represented their life savings. I can still to this day remember the faces of those victims as they described their despair over losing what they had worked a lifetime to accumulate.

I interviewed one woman in her mobile home located just outside of Camas, Washington. She had spent her entire life working for the paper bag company in Camas and had managed to save $39,000 for her retirement. She was attracted to Desert Investments because they were offering high interest rates and they claimed the investments were secure. She invested all $39,000 with the company and lost it all. I just cannot describe the anguish I felt for her and the deep sense of helplessness over not being able to get her back her money.

In the meantime, two weeks after filing bankruptcy in Washington State, the principals of the firm moved ten miles south to Portland and opened a new fraudulent investment firm. This was the most frustrating thing I had ever been through. We had thrown everything we had at this company and we not only failed to recover investors' money, but we barely even slowed the principals down. It was the last fraud case I ever worked on.

Since that time, I have been absolutely driven by the notion of getting to older adults before the con artists do and teaching them how to avoid being victims of fraud. That is why in 1993 I went to work for the American Association of Retired Persons (AARP) as the economic security/consumer representative for the states of Washington, Oregon, Idaho, and Alaska. It is also what this book is all about.

John T., who has collaborated with me on this book, has a background that is precisely the opposite of mine. While I spent the 1980s chasing after con artists, John was ripping off as many people as he could throughout the United States. I heard about John while attending a conference of senior newspaper editors in San Diego, California. Attorney General Ken Eikenberry and I did a presentation on fraud against the elderly along with a detective from the San Diego District Attorney's office. The detective told me he had a two-hour videotape of a phone fraud guy they had busted. He said his name was John T., and he was telling a group of law enforcement people about the business as his way of helping curtail the fraud problem.

I told the detective we were about to film a video about senior adult fraud and would love to see the tape and possibly contact John T. to volunteer to be part of the project.

After seeing this rather crude videotape which was made with a home video recorder held rather unsteadily by a San Diego police officer, I was certain John was our man.

The first time I talked to John, we had a two-and-a-half-hour-long conversation and, oddly enough, quickly became friends (a stranger pair you will never find!). He was the first true con artist I had ever met who was willing to admit his wrongdoings. And even though I had spent my entire professional life despising people like him, I realized he could be the key to a very effective strategy to prevent fraud.

Every case I ever worked on involved the testimony of former employees who could tell us what was going on inside the operation. I believed that John's value to our efforts was that he could reveal what was going on inside boiler rooms all across the country and provide rare insight into the methods of con artists. This is precisely what he has done both in Washington State's crime prevention efforts and in this book.

John was arguably one of the best phone fraud operators in the United States at the time he was caught. He started out in a phone room in Las Vegas which later became the "Grandaddy" of all phone operations, with over 350 salespeople calling nationwide. He quickly became the top salesperson in that phone room, and whenever the state or the federal government was about to close in on a room he would skip town and move to another state where he found instant employment with another fraud operation.

John was so good at the phone fraud game that he became a trainer of young phone room operators, traveling the country teaching "rookie" frauders the tricks of the trade. He was revered by phone room people throughout the country as the "king of the phone room" because he could sell anything to anyone.

"I did kind of get to the point of feeling invincible," John said in a recent interview. "I would take bets from guys that I could make up a ridiculous product and sell it. One time I bet some guys I could sell tickets for the first civilian-manned space shuttle mission in 1998. Those tickets sold like hotcakes!"

After defrauding America for ten years, the only reason John got caught is because an eleven-agency federal task force decided to crack down on telemarketing fraud in Southern California in a massive expenditure of manpower and resources . . . and because John got overly self-confident.

"I knew the task force was looking for us at the time of my bust. Heck, two months before I was arrested, they had busted another room I was in. I got away because I pretended I was just an innocent young man trying to make my way in life and didn't know what we were doing was illegal. They bought that and only arrested the owner of the room.

"Normally, when that kind of heat comes down, I would be on the next plane to the East Coast. But I had gotten away with it for so long that I decided to just move one city up the line. I even used the same mailing list of people we had been calling at the time of the first bust. I felt untouchable, like no one could stop me, not even a federal task force—I was wrong!"

Notwithstanding his mistake, John did a grand total of sixty days in jail and was ordered to pay back $120,000 in restitution. Instead of training delinquent teenagers in the phone fraud business John has worked with me, the Washington State Attorney General's office, and other government agencies as an unpaid consultant, training consumers how the pitches work so they can avoid victimization.

In 1990 we launched a statewide fraud prevention program for older persons called the "Stop Fraud Network." This program involved every major senior adult organization in the state. We featured John in a twenty-three-minute video entitled *The Stop Fraud Documentary,* in which he reenacted sales pitches directed toward older consumers he used while working in fraud phone rooms around the nation. The video also contains other reenactments such as the bank examiner, Medigap insurance, and equity skimming scams.

A key part of the program was public speaking. I traveled to every corner of the state giving fraud prevention speeches to senior centers, American Association of Retired Persons groups, retired teachers, and the like. We also enlisted the help of volunteer "fraud fighters" whom I trained to be familiar with fraud pitches targeting older adults. These volunteer "fraud fighters" (many of them retired teachers or local AARP chapter members) then took the video out into the community and showed it to senior groups.

Over a two-year period, over 3 million people had seen some or all of the *Stop Fraud* video's material. The Stop Fraud Network won two national awards in 1991 for innovative government programming, including "Consumer Education Program of the Year in the Nation" given by the National Association of Consumer Agency Administrators (NACAA).

This book is a natural extension of the Stop Fraud Network. We were amazed at the interest in this topic around the country. Law enforcement departments and consumer agencies from every state in the country have requested information about our fraud prevention materials and the Stop Fraud Network.

The information in this book represents the collective knowledge John and I have accumulated over twenty-five years of combined experience (from both sides of the law) on the issue of fraud. We believe it represents a unique and comprehensive view of the tricks used by con artists to victimize older persons.

While the book has been written in my voice, John T.'s input in this process over the past four years has been the key to many of the insights contained herein. I have learned more from him about fraud during this time than I learned in the previous ten years as a fraud investigator.

All of the companies', victims', and con artists' names have been changed to protect the innocent (and the guilty). This includes my writing partner, John T., who is seeking to return to a normal, honest life and does not believe the notoriety of this book will improve his chances of finding legitimate employment in the future.

I believe that every older person who reads this book will greatly reduce his or her chances of becoming a fraud victim. Our intention is not to make people unduly fearful or cynical. Rather, it is to level the playing field and, for the first time, give consumers access to the same information about con artists as con artists have about them. With thousands of American consumers armed with detailed information about con artists and their craft, it can then be said, "Let the buyer *and seller* beware."

THE STORY OF EMMA

Although certain names and locations have been changed, the following account is based on a real story of victimization that occurred while this book was being completed in the spring of 1993. The author has decided to open the book with it because it is such a dramatic example of how ruthless con artists can be, how devastating the results can be for the victim, and how something can be done if friends and relatives of the victim intervene and take action.

—Editor's Note

Emma was the switchboard operator at the Sand Point Naval Air Station in Seattle for almost twenty-five years. She and her husband raised a daughter and while they were certainly not rich, Emma kept all the books throughout their forty-five-year marriage and was very good at saving money, as were many of her generation.

Emma and her husband Bob retired with good pensions from their jobs and a significant nest egg which was invested in mutual funds, insurance annuities, and other sensible, safe investment vehicles.

In March 1991, Bob died after a rather lengthy illness. For the first time in forty-five years, Emma was alone. Her daughter Karen had long since moved away and was living in Alaska; Emma had a few friends but saw them infrequently. And because at eighty-four years of age she could no longer drive, it was difficult to get out to a senior center or other place to meet new people her own age.

Soon after her husband's death, to keep herself busy, Emma began to open junk mail. Although it had always come to their home, while Bob was alive it had been ignored. One flyer read:

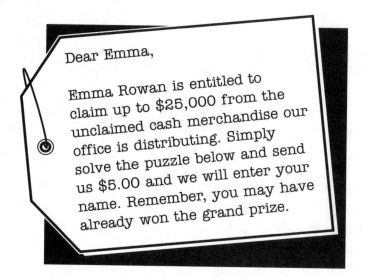

Dear Emma,

Emma Rowan is entitled to claim up to $25,000 from the unclaimed cash merchandise our office is distributing. Simply solve the puzzle below and send us $5.00 and we will enter your name. Remember, you may have already won the grand prize.

Emma decided that it would be awfully nice to win $25,000. Also, she found that she could solve the puzzle easily . . . and $5.00 wasn't much to risk, so she filled out the form and sent it in, listing her current phone number on the form so that she could be promptly notified if she won.

For the first couple of months, Emma sent in a couple of these forms per week. As time went on however, she found that opening the mail, solving the puzzles, and sending the forms was kind of a fun activity, or at least something to occupy her time. She noticed that the more forms she filled out, the more were sent to her.

Soon she began getting telephone calls from very friendly-sounding people who were calling her to tell her that she had done very well in the promotion she had entered. They told her that she had won at least $5,000 worth of merchandise or cash and as much as $30,000 or a brand new car.

The only catch was that she would have to send them $599 for a two-year supply of vitamins or $499 for some cleaning liquid. But that wasn't too much to pay for winning at least $5,000, was it?

Then some people started calling her and telling her she had won a fabulous prize and all she had to do was donate $2,000 to the "Just Say No to Drugs" campaign they were working on to keep kids on the straight and narrow. "That's a good cause," Emma said to herself thinking of her own two grandchildren who were nine and thirteen years old.

Over time Emma began to get so much mail and so many phone calls that she was unable to leave her house except to go to the store for groceries. She was writing literally hundreds of checks per month for as little as $3.00 and as much as $5,000. She began to realize that she wasn't winning the grand prize and that mostly what she won were bracelets or small televisions sets, always the smallest of the prize options which the telemarketers listed when they called.

After about a year, Karen visited her one day and became outraged that Emma was "throwing her money away" by buying things over the phone. To remedy matters, while Emma was visiting a friend, Karen decided she was going to solve the problem of telemarketers stealing her mother's money. She threw away all of Emma's paperwork that had anything to do with sweepstakes or prize giveaways and she changed her phone number—all without asking Emma.

When she returned, Emma was furious that her daughter had interfered with her business in that way. The two had words over it and for the next year Emma and Karen did not speak to each other. Other attempts by her friends had also proved fruitless. Emma was truly hooked by the sweepstakes mentality.

By the late spring of 1993, some two years after Bob had died and she had begun to play these so-called "games of chance" promotions through the mail and over the phone, Emma was feeling trapped. She couldn't seem to stop writing checks or answering her phone, yet she realized that she was losing the nest egg she and her husband had worked a lifetime to accumulate. Her mailbox was now filled every day with more sweepstakes promotions—sometimes twenty-five to thirty pieces in a single day. The telemarketers were calling every hour on the hour. Sometimes the telephone rooms would send Emma a dozen roses on her birthday to thank her.

During the time she was participating in these promotions, she had come to be acquainted with a woman who delivered the Federal Express packages to her and also picked up checks that were headed for Las Vegas and other telephone rooms around the country. One day, this woman named Julie stopped long enough to ask Emma if she was sure she knew what she was doing by sending all these checks to telemarketers. Emma thanked her for her concern, but indicated that she was about to quit because all of the callers had told her it was the final promotion of the summer and then they wouldn't call anymore.

Julie was unconvinced that the calls would stop coming, so while she was delivering a package to the local AARP office, she stopped in and spoke to me. Given my background with consumer fraud and the attorney general's office, I became immediately concerned that Emma was indeed being ripped off.

I called Emma and explained to her who I was and that Julie had been worried about her. Emma claimed that she had been involved with telemarketers but that it was all about to end. I told her I was only a mile away and asked if she would mind if I came over to talk to her. Emma agreed to let me visit her, but she said it would have to be after 10:00 A.M. because she had to go to the bank the next morning.

When I arrived the next morning, I was amazed at what I found. Emma's house looked like a warehouse for telemarketers. In looking through her checkbook, I found that she had written 2,500 checks of various amounts since January 1992. She had written checks totaling $141,500 since January 1993, and she had written $48,000 worth of checks in the past thirty days! Emma then took me down to her garage which was also full of boxes. When I decided I was going to have to help her send some of these boxes back, I inventoried them and found that she had over eighty boxes full of televisions, pens, pencils, fake jewelry, microwave ovens, paintings, etc. Emma, I thought to myself, was the worst victim of telemarketing I had ever seen.

I immediately set out to try and unwind some of the transactions Emma had gotten herself into. As I looked through the checkbook, pulling out the bigger checks, I was shocked to realize that in many cases, Emma could not remember writing the check even though she had recorded it in her check register. She had written a check for $9,807 to some firm in Houston, $4,990 to another firm in Las Vegas, $6,000 to a firm in Buffalo, New York, and couldn't remember what she got for any of them.

As I started piecing together checks with company names and merchandise in her house and garage, I began to see the picture emerge of how these telemarketers were getting to Emma:

First she would fill out the entry form in the mail and send it in. (This mail is usually sent by the telemarketer or by a lead generation firm which sells the names of people like Emma to them, complete with a phone number so they can call her.) Then the telemarketer would place a follow-up call and tell Emma she had won one of four fabulous prizes: a new Cadillac worth $35,000, $10,000 in cash, a trip to Europe, or a nineteen-inch color television.

All she had to do was buy a two-year supply of liquid cleaner (six gallons for $2,000) or make a donation to keep kids off drugs and they would send her award certificate indicating what she had won. They would send an overnight delivery runner out to the house that day to pick up the check and that was that.

It is this basic pitch that Emma fell for over and over again. I counted seventy-five Federal Express receipts in her house along with several other overnight delivery company receipts. When it was all said and done, I figured Emma had spent $220,000—her life savings. And what did she have to show for it? A garage full of pens and pencils, Frisbees that say "Say No to Drugs," liquid soap, and fake diamond necklaces.

I immediately reverted back to my former role as a fraud investigator and opened an investigative file on every telemarketer to whom Emma had written a check. The only problem was that there were so many checks, I had to ignore any firm to whom she had paid less than $500. Even so, I had twenty-seven files—twenty-seven different firms that had ripped off this eighty-four-year-old widow for at least $500 during an eighteen-month period.

While I was visiting Emma that first day, the phone rang several times. The first call was from a firm in Buffalo. The telemarketer was calling Emma back to see if she had been able to do what he said and go to the bank and borrow $5,000 in order to be able to participate in his promotion. It seems that when Emma told him that she had no money left, he asked her if she owned her home. When she said she did, he told her (not asked her, but told her) to go down to the bank and take out an equity loan. I suddenly realized that was why Emma could not meet me first thing that morning, because she was applying for an equity loan to give to a telemarketer from Buffalo. I abruptly took the phone from Emma's hand at that point and demanded the firm refund the other $5,000 Emma had already sent them or I would turn them in to the FBI. They complied.

For two weeks after that first meeting, I made it my priority to call these telemarketers who had ripped off Emma and threaten to turn them in if they didn't refund her money. Because Emma had spent so much in the preceding thirty days, I was relatively successful at getting some of the money back. Any money that had been sent more than two or three months before, however, was gone. Each telemarketing firm said basically the same thing in response to my calls: we are not like those other firms that rip people off. We sent out the products, we delivered the prizes we said we'd deliver, and therefore we are legitimate. When I confronted them with the fact that Emma paid in one case $6,000 for six one-gallon containers of liquid soap and won a nineteen-inch color television worth about $200, the phone room operator said, "Hey, before we sent her the stuff, we called and confirmed her order and she agreed on tape that she was happy with it. Then we sent her the product and the gift. Not only that, we gave her a thirty-day money back guarantee along with the products. Now, three months later, you come along and convince her she made a bad deal 'cause she paid too much for the soap—too bad pal."

I had been through the drill before. I knew that these telemarketers were smart and that Emma didn't have a leg to stand on legally, even though she couldn't remember writing many of the checks she had sent and therefore there was an issue about whether she was capable of entering into a binding contract.

I had many screaming matches with telemarketers over a two-week period. One of the last conversations I had was with a phone room owner who had been in the business for ten years and was extremely belligerent. After the owner had refused to refund any of the $20,000 he had stolen from Emma, I asked him why he seemed to pick on vulnerable little old ladies. He said, "Hey, it's not my fault if they're stupid. The only way you're going to stop this from happening is by teaching these little old ladies not to fall for my pitches."

I realized that the phone room owner was exactly right. These rooms have virtually airtight legal arguments for what they are doing and the only way to stop older people from losing their life savings is by teaching them about how the scams operate. The moral of the story is that what happened to Emma could happen to you. She is a bright, independent, financially savvy person, who happened to get a little lonely after her husband died. Out of grief and loneliness, she got involved in something that gave her something to do, people to talk to, flowers on special occasions and, she thought, the chance to win big prizes.

There are thousands of Emmas out there in America. Congressional studies estimate that older persons lose billions of dollars each year to telemarketing scams of one kind or another. Billions more are lost to mail fraud, door-to-door scams, and a variety of others.

But you don't have to be a victim. The material in this book is designed to teach you how to identify scams of all kinds, learn who the con artists target as victims, and discover how to prevent these scams from happening to you. And you don't have to be a former fraud investigator to intervene and help older people when you see them being victimized. In the end, I was able to get $75,000 back for Emma by making dozens of phone calls and helping her return some of the eighty boxes she had accumulated. You can become an American fraud fighter and intervene on behalf of family and friends so they don't fall prey to greedy telemarketers.

By the way, Emma has stopped taking phone calls from scam artists now. She politely says "No thank you" and immediately hangs up. She changed her phone number—this time of her own volition. She put a new wastebasket by the front door and every morning she sorts her mail while standing there. All the sweepstakes offers and solicitations go into that trash basket—unopened.

Emma and Karen are talking again. Karen convinced her mother to get out more often. They arranged to have a local shuttle service pick Emma up several times a week and take her to the local senior center. She's making new friends and renewing her interests in such subjects as Oriental art.

Emma looks back on those two years as a nightmare. She will never recover the money she lost. And her dignity and self-assurance are badly bruised. But if Emma's story can keep one person from suffering as she did, she says it's worth the humiliation.

So, the next time a telephone caller or an official-looking letter tempts you to send off for a prize "you've already won," remember Emma's story.

CHAPTER

2

QUESTIONS AND ANSWERS ABOUT FRAUD

"Interesting things are never true . . . and the truth is only convincing when it is told by an experienced liar."

—John Oliver Holmes

Between 1988 and 1992, I gave over three hundred speeches about fraud to some 17,000 older citizens in 125 communities. The settings for these speeches varied: from as few as five elderly women members of a Philanthropic Education Organization meeting in the cramped living room of one of its members to 1,000 people at Gonzaga University for a "Senior Day" health fair.

Other settings for these presentations included AARP chapter meetings held in a senior center, retired teacher meetings, and senior kiwanis meetings, which were typically held in community centers or restaurants. During this period of time, no location was too remote and no group too small. I once drove 120 miles to Wenatchee to speak to an evening meeting of senior kiwanians that had five people in attendance. As a consequence, I was driving 25,000 to 30,000 miles per year to reach the most remote locations of the state.

The typical person attending these meetings was an older consumer between the ages of sixty and eighty. Most attended meetings and belonged to organizations as a way to socialize with friends, stay active and, importantly, stay informed.

Over time, I came to realize that people who belong to these types of organizations are much less likely to be the victims of fraud; not necessarily because they heard me speak but because the social contact and interaction with others helped them avoid two major causes of victimization: loneliness and boredom.

Although the settings for these speeches differed widely, one thing was the same everywhere: the questions from the audience. From the urban senior centers of Seattle to the rustic cafés of Colville and Dayton, older consumers all seemed to want to know the same things. What follows are the most commonly asked questions and the answers I gave after my speeches. They are in no particular order.

 "As someone over sixty-five years of age, am I more likely to be a fraud victim than a younger person?"

Statistically, you are more likely to be the victim of fraud. Studies have shown that while older people comprise 12 to 13 percent of the U.S. population, they comprise 30 percent of all the victims of fraud and 60 percent of all the victims of health fraud.

And while these statistics imply that seniors are targets for con artists, it is by no means a given that every older person will become a fraud victim. In fact, the assumption underlying the Stop Fraud Network, our massive outreach efforts over the years, and this book has been that learning how con games work can prevent victimization.

"Why are older persons the biggest target for con artists?"

Con artists are like most criminals. They are lazy. They don't want to work hard to accomplish their goals. You might say they follow the path of least resistance. Unfortunately, older persons often represent the path of least resistance for a variety of reasons:

1. Accessibility

Older persons, unlike busy baby boomers and other two-income families, are available to the con artist. They are home during the day, they go shopping at the grocery store, and so on. This makes them prime targets for telemarketers like John or the door-to-door home repair con man.

2. Social isolation

Because the rest of the world is so busy and seniors are retired, they often find themselves socially isolated and lonely. According to recent Census Bureau statistics, close to one-third of all seniors over age sixty-five live alone. And of those, almost 80 percent are women.

The combination of isolation, which makes older consumers willing to talk to anyone, including con artists, and lack of education or experience with finances, makes women a big target.

There are many agencies and organizations which offer special courses and services for older women on the issue of financial decision-making. AARP in particular offers the Woman's Financial Information Program, a seven-week course designed to empower women to take control of their finances. In addition, community colleges and university extension offices offer financial training for women.

These courses are especially valuable for recently divorced or widowed women like Emma, who was profiled in the last chapter. Even though Emma was knowledgeable about the basics of financial decision-making, when her husband died she became distraught and needed a support mechanism. Often, such classes serve the dual function of providing information and new friendships with people who are in similar life circumstances.

3. Declining mental and physical conditions

Sometimes seniors are easy prey simply because of declining mental functions (see the Alzheimer's pitch in chapter 3). Men in particular are reluctant to acknowledge such decline and are all the more vulnerable as a result.

4. Seniors have money

The other thing that makes older persons a target is that they have money to steal. Most have worked a lifetime to accumulate assets like home equity, savings accounts, and pension income. Con artists do their market research and the first rule of any salesmanship is "sell only to those with the money to buy." Seniors are also naturally distrustful of banking, having come from the Depression era when many banks failed. Consequently, they tend to keep large amounts of cash on hand.

 "If I suspect that I am being approached by a con artist, what should I do? Won't he hurt me if I turn him away?"

One of the most common fears older persons have is that they will be confronted by a criminal and due to natural human frailty or physical weakness, will be injured or even killed.

While it is true that there are people who would mug their own grandmother for money, the statistics show older persons are less frequent victims of violent crime than younger people.

And when it comes to con artists, my experience is that they are not violent. If you turn away a home repair contractor whom you suspect is a con man, the chances are very good that he will simply go on to the next house rather than assaulting you in any way.

The reason for this is simple. Con artists are smarter than your average mugger or bank robber. They know that if they engage in a "crime against person," the police are going to come after them.

If however, they simply pretend to be a legitimate business like a home repair contractor, then it is a civil matter. This means the police consider your dealings with the con artist to be a contractual dispute, not a crime. And even if he does rip you off, it is a "crime against property" which is given a much lower priority by the police department than crimes against people.

Therefore, if you suspect the person on the phone or at your door or in the parking lot is a swindler, simply hang up or turn him away. Remember, con artists follow the path of least resistance. If you put up any resistance, they will likely leave you alone.

 "How do con artists get my name in the first place?"

We live in an information age. You would be amazed at the information available about you. For example, I could go downtown to a marketing firm and purchase a list of five thousand older adults living in Bellevue, Washington, who are retired and who have at least $50,000 annual retirement income. The list would include their name, address, phone number and would cost between $300 to $500.

It is important to realize that when the phone rings, often the caller knows a lot more about you than you know about him or her.

Think about the information available to anyone in a public library. As investigators, city directories are a tool we use all the time to find people. A city directory is a thick book compiled by private firms who go door to door throughout neighborhoods collecting detailed information about residents on each street. If you were a con artist wanting to steal the equity in a person's home, the first thing you might do is look in the city directory. And what does it tell you about any given person? It lists the name, how long the person lived there, whether or not the person owns the home, and the person's occupation.

So the con artist sees an entry for Hazel Smith. She has lived in her home, which she owns, for thirty-five years, and she is listed as retired. It is also significant what the entry does not say . . . there is no husband listed.

In all likelihood, the con artist concludes, this Hazel Smith is the perfect target for the equity skimming con (see chapter 3). She is a widow, living alone and retired, who has probably paid off the mortgage and is sitting on a ton of equity.

Another source of information are lists generated by magazine subscriptions, credit card accounts, gas cards, and the like. Some magazines make more money selling the lists of their subscribers than they do from the subscriptions themselves.

Part of the reason why magazine subscriptions are so valuable as a marketing tool is because they target the consumer. For example, if you subscribe to a monthly publication called *I Love to Travel Magazine* (I made this up), this tells us something about you and everyone else who subscribes to that publication—you love to travel.

If I were a travel agency, don't you think it would be worth something to me to buy the list of all the people who subscribe to *I Love to Travel Magazine*? Of course it would.

The one list which you really want to try to avoid is the "mooch" list. Mooch is a rather derogatory term for a consumer who "wants something for nothing." It is a term used in telemarketing fraud boiler rooms across the country.

The way you get on a mooch list is by falling for one of the many free prize pitches for which con artists are so famous. Anyone who responds to contests sent through the mail risks getting on a "mooch" list. The contest might say something like:

Dear Diane,

Solve the puzzle below and send $5.00 to enter your name as a contestant to win the $25,000 grand prize.

I interviewed a con artist from a boiler room in Las Vegas who said these mail scams are not done to get $5.00 from victims. As he said, "That is just chump change. But if they fall for a small scam, they'll fall for bigger ones." In Vegas and other areas across the United States, telemarketing boiler rooms will buy and sell lead lists comprised of people who have innocently entered these contests.

Once you have demonstrated your willingness to fall for the "something for nothing" pitch, watch out. The telemarketers will call you until you have spent your last dime. Phone room operators buy, sell, and trade mooch lists frequently so that it is never the same voice on the other end of the phone.

I interviewed an elderly victim of telemarketers last year who had gotten onto a mooch list. This woman met the criteria for the most vulnerable older adult. She was a ninety-one-year-old widow living alone.

It seems her daughter was visiting her from California one day and started to go through her checkbook. She noticed there were several checks written to Choice Marketing in Las Vegas for $499 and another check for $599 to Quality Enterprises in Miami. When she totaled up the checks, she discovered her mother had spent over $7,000 in the preceding twelve months on telemarketers.

Each time the pitch was roughly the same: "You have won either $10,000 in cash, a new car, a trip to Europe, or a toaster." In order to find out which prize she had won, however, she had to buy $500 worth of vitamins which they claimed normally sold for $1,000. As soon as she agreed to buy, they sent an overnight express runner out to the house to pick up the check.

When I interviewed her in her home, she had twenty-two different express delivery receipts. Twenty-two times telemarketers had pitched her, sold her, and sent the express runner out to take her money.

When I asked this woman, who seemed otherwise quite intelligent, why she had continued to fall for these pitches, she said "the deeper the hole I dug for myself, the more I wanted to believe I had really won when the next call came."

She was, in effect, throwing good money after bad in an attempt to become whole financially. She was a textbook victim of the sweepstakes mentality. Avoid getting on mooch lists.

"How can I get my name off of these lists?"

It is very difficult to get your name off of lists once you are on them. Many people feel angry about the amount of junk mail they receive each month. They feel it is not only an invasion of privacy, but amounts to mailbox pollution. The problem is balancing the right to privacy with the first amendment freedom to express yourself and advertise your business.

There is an organization called the Direct Mail Marketer's Association located in Washington, DC, to which many direct mail companies belong. You can write to them and say you wish to be taken off of all mailing lists used by their members and they will accommodate your request. Their address is 1101 17th Street, NW, Suite 705, Washington, DC 20036.

It should be pointed out however that there are many hundreds of direct mail companies which are not members of this association and therefore will not take you off their list.

 "I get a lot of calls from charities wanting my money. How do I know if they are legitimate?"

There are literally tens of thousands of nonprofit organizations raising money at any one time throughout the United States. Many states have a charitable solicitation law which requires any organization raising money above a certain threshold amount in a year to be registered with the state.

Once a year, the registered organizations must fill out financial disclosure forms which list the fund-raising activities in which they have engaged during the year. This disclosure must include a summary of how much of the money they raised actually went to the charitable purpose versus the fund-raiser.

If you are called and asked to give money to a charity, you should ask the caller to send you a written statement about the charity, its purpose, and history. Included with that written information should be the registration number listed with the state and a written statement of what percentage of the money the charity takes in goes to the charity versus the fund-raiser.

While most charities which raise money are legitimate, there are some whose primary charitable purpose is themselves. There are really two kinds of problem charitable solicitors:

1. Bogus charities

I have worked on cases in which the professional fund-raiser keeps 100 percent of the money he or she raises. The so-called charity was created simply as a tool to raise money. Quite often, these bogus charities will be tied to a news event such as a flood, earthquake, recent crime wave, or war.

In 1972, when the Arab oil embargo was supposedly causing long gas lines (I say "supposedly" because the attorneys general of seven states claimed the major oil companies were contriving the oil shortage), a young law student started marketing the "Maximum Efficiency Calibrator." This device, which cost $19.95, was guaranteed to cut your gas bill in half. At a time when all of us were getting up at 5:00 A.M. to wait in line for gasoline, this was an attractive offer. Hundreds of people paid the $19.95.

What did they receive for their money? A one-inch square block of wood and instructions to place the block of wood underneath the car's accelerator, thereby enabling the driver to compress the gas pedal only 50 percent of the way to the floor thereby saving him or her 50 percent on the gas bill.

In May 1980, when Mt. St. Helens erupted, I was sent down to the disaster relief center in Kelso, Washington, to help victims of this catastrophic natural disaster. While we were down there, we discovered a guy selling buttons which had a felt-tip marker drawing of the state of Washington with an erupting Mt. St. Helens on it for $15—all proceeds to benefit the Toutle Lake Disaster Relief Fund. Sorry, fella. It seems this was nothing more than a way for a young entrepreneur to take advantage of the disaster.

In 1991 when war broke out in the Middle East, we had numerous charities emerge: Civilians who Support Desert Storm Troops, the Persian Gulf Relief Fund and many more. The reason these bogus charities were tied to news events is because the news legitimizes the sales pitch.

For example, you're sitting home all day long watching CNN's coverage of the gulf war effort. Perhaps you're a veteran yourself, wishing you could help the effort somehow. But how? All of a sudden, the phone rings and it's a representative from "Citizens who Support Desert Storm Troops" wanting a $100 donation to help our guys and gals overseas.

We sued the operator of such bogus Desert Storm charities and found that he had raised almost $600,000 from nine different fake charities. Where did the money go? To pay his mortgage; to buy his girlfriend a bigger diamond ring; to make the payments on his new Ferrari. You get the picture. Virtually all of the money was converted to his own use.

2. Fund-raisers who keep most of the money

Another problem in the charitable giving area has to do with professional fund-raisers who keep a large percentage of the money they raise for a legitimate charity. Let's take the example of law enforcement.

People will give an unlimited amount of money to feel safer. The reason is they see reports on the news every night of the rising crime rates, the riots in Los Angeles, etc. Older persons can become especially fearful of such reports.

So here is what can happen. Professional fund-raisers will come into your community and find out who runs the local police guild. They will approach that person(s) and state that they are professional fund-raisers. One of the fund-raisers asks, "How would you like a cashier's check for $5,000 right now?"

The police guild person says something like, "It's hard to raise money and sure we would love $5,000, but what's the catch?"

"Oh there is no catch. All you have to do is sign this piece of paper authorizing us to use your name in fund-raising for the next thirty days and we will give you a cashier's check for $5,000 right now!"

Fund-raisers will then set up a boiler room operation and from 4:00 P.M. until 9:00 P.M. every night, call citizens in the community, and say something like:

"Hi I'm calling from the local police guild and we are raising money to help the police department stop that terrible crime problem—by the way did

you hear about the assault that occurred last Saturday night—how about a $100 contribution?"

They might raise as much as $100,000 during that thirty-day period and then leave town. They only promised to pay the guild $5,000 which they did in advance, but they raised $100,000! This means that ninety-five cents of every dollar raised for the purpose of keeping the community safe left town.

This is why it is so important to get written information from the fund-raisers and require them to provide a breakdown of how the money is being distributed. If you knew that of every $100 contribution you made, only $5.00 of it was actually going to the charity, would you still give it? I know I wouldn't.

 "Are all con artists men?"

Absolutely not. Some of the most effective con artists are women who prey on men. Let me give you an example. Last year, the daughter of a senior called the local AARP office to report her father had been the victim of a female con artist. The AARP office referred her to me.

It seems that this person (who we will call Carol) had gone to visit her father (who we will call Jim). Carol got to talking to her father and he told her about a young woman named Barbara whom he found sitting on his front porch one day when he returned from the grocery store.

Carol told me her father lives in a mobile home, is seventy-three years old, widowed, but up until two years ago, he had been a very active, physically strong man. He was a logger by trade and up until his seventy-first birthday had enjoyed hiking and snow skiing. His health had started to decline when he was diagnosed as having Parkison's disease. This led to him feeling less self-confident and, she believes, contributed to his vulnerability with this woman.

Jim told Carol that when he asked what this girl was doing, she told him the sad story of her recent past: her mother and father and only brother had all died in the past six months, she had very low self-esteem because she had crooked teeth and was unattractive, and her day-care business was on the brink of going under.

Jim felt sympathetic and invited Barbara into his trailer for tea. As Carol later described it, Jim found that he enjoyed Barbara's company and wanted to help her. Within two hours of meeting, Barbara was leading Jim down to his bank to withdraw $600 in cash to give her so she could put braces on her teeth.

When Jim's daughter discovered what he had done, she confronted him. Jim said the girl was having some bad luck and would pay him back when she got back on her feet. When Carol called Barbara to confront her, she denied taking any money from Jim at all.

"I just like his company," Barbara said. "We're just friends."

Over the next couple of weeks, Barbara continued to call on Jim, taking him shopping and to the movies. Carol continued to be concerned for her father's welfare and decided to call on him more often. She tried to discourage him from seeing Barbara, but he refused to stop seeing her. It was at that point that Carol called the AARP office and subsequently spoke to me. Unfortunately, by the time she called, the situation had worsened dramatically.

"I found that my father had given this woman a total of $24,000. In addition to getting him to withdraw $600 here and $1,000 there, she actually drove him to Mount Vernon to collect a $16,000 debt owed to him," Carol told me.

It short, con women are not only out there, they are arguably more dangerous especially to older men because they can use flirtation, sympathy, and charm to endear themselves to the victim. You might say consumer fraud victims never met a con artist they didn't like.

 "Is it dangerous to fill out questionnaires that come in the mail or surveys conducted over the phone?"

There are legitimate telemarketing firms which are doing research for universities and private companies, or polling for political candidates. Some telemarketing firms even offer to (and do) give you a gift if you answer their questions.

You begin to run into problems when the caller is posing as a research firm in order to gain information about you which can later be used to rip you off.

For example, last year I was speaking to a retirement group about telemarketing fraud. A woman raised her hand and told the group about a call she had received recently:

"I received a call from a person claiming to be from ABC Research Company. She said they were taking a survey to find out what kind of products consumers used in their homes. I agreed to answer her questions, thinking it was harmless enough. She then asked the following questions:

① What kind of laundry detergent to you use?
② What kind of dishwashing soap do you use?
③ Do you own a VCR? If so, what kind?
④ What kind of garbage bags do you use?
⑤ How many television sets do you own? What kind?
⑥ Do you work outside of the home? If so when to you work? 8-5? 12-9?

I can't prove it, but I think this woman was posing as a research firm in order to case my house, find out what I had that she could steal, and determine when I would be at work so she could come and burglarize me."

I must admit that was the first time I had heard of such a scam, but I had to agree that the questions sounded pretty suspicious.

The bottom line is that if you feel uncomfortable with questions being asked over the phone, say you're not interested in participating and hang up. So many times, I have heard people say they continued to listen to a telemarketer or answer survey questions because they didn't want to be rude. Yet so many times, the call comes during the dinner hour when most people are home. I think that is pretty rude.

You are free to fill out cards which ask if you would like more information about "how to save thousands of dollars by avoiding the agony of probate," for example. Just realize that salespersons call these "lead cards" and it will undoubtedly result in a salesperson calling on you to sell you a living trust, insurance, or some other product.

Another approach used by salespersons is to encourage shoppers at the mall to fill out a card in order to enter a drawing to win a prize. Remember our discussion about the mooch lists? You provide your name, address, and phone number and it will almost certainly result in a salesperson calling you or even showing up at your door unannounced.

 "Is it ever true that I really have won a prize or are they all scams? What about sweepstakes-type promotions that claim I may have won $10 million?"

All of these promotions prey on the "sweepstakes mentality": the idea that you can get something very valuable for nothing, or at least something valuable for very little.

Having handled thousands of consumer complaints and hundreds of investigations, and having spoken to groups about these types of promotions for the past thirteen years, it is very tempting for me to say "they are all scams." The whole notion that "if it sounds too good to be true, it probably is" really applies here.

Why would a firm in business to make money be willing to give away a brand new car or $10,000 in cash? Those promoters who walk the thin line between fraud and mere misleading advertising will usually give away one car for every 100,000 people who sign up. Signing up can mean anything from listening to a sales pitch to buying a camping club or discount vitamins.

The next time you receive a "prize award notification" sales pitch in the mail, look on the back at the fine print. Semi-legitimate direct mail firms will disclose (in very small print) that the chance of you winning the grand prize is about one in 100,000. The chance of you winning the clock radio is 99,997 in 100,000. And by the way, you will have to pay $19.95 for shipping and handling.

With regard to the sweepstakes-type promotion, they do not violate the law as far as I am aware. Furthermore, they do in fact give away a million-dollar prize as advertised.

The reason they can afford to give away that kind of money is that they sell a lot of magazines through this promotion. In direct mail marketing, the whole key to profitability is response rate. By getting a nationally known figure to go on television and suggest that you may have won $10 million and all you have to do is open the sweepstakes promotion envelope when it comes in the mail and send it in, this company increases its response rate tremendously.

Most state laws say it is illegal to have to buy something in order to enter a contest or drawing. Therefore, Publisher's Clearinghouse does not require consumers to purchase magazines in order to enter their promotion to win the $10 million.

However, they are banking on the fact that if you are going to take the time to open the envelope, find the one form (among numerous other complicated forms) which you can fill out without purchasing magazines, the chances are you are going to also order at least one magazine.

I am asked about the Publisher's Clearinghouse promotion almost every time I give a speech. One time, a lady stood up after we had discussed it and she said, "I always thought that the more magazines I ordered, the better my chances of winning." Even though the solicitation does not state this, one could easily get the same wrong impression this lady had and order more magazines than one would otherwise in order to increase the chances of winning the $10 million.

These high-visibility promotions which stay just this side of the line between legality and illegality give rise to out-and-out scam artists exploiting the sweepstakes mentality by promising huge prizes, then selling overpriced water filters or vitamins.

I have often said in speeches that state-sponsored lotteries also fuel the sweepstakes mentality and should be banned altogether. Just like the sweepstakes-type promotion, they prey on a citizen's desire to get something for nothing and they indirectly sanction or give credibility to scam artists who use the same pitch and provide little in return.

 "Have you ever had problems with religious organizations financially victimizing their members?"

I think the vast majority of churches and religious organizations in the United States are outstanding and provide remarkable levels of spiritual guidance and service to their members and especially to indigent populations.

Having said that, if I were to ever lose my sense of right and wrong and decide to start a scam, I would become an evangelic preacher. As a religious organization, I would be exempt from property taxes and income taxes, there would be a widespread presumption by the general public that I was squeaky clean and, most importantly, the constitutional separation of church and state would make it nearly impossible for law enforcement organizations to investigate me.

As an investigator, I ran up against this constitutional problem all the time with organizations claiming the religious organization status. In one example, I tried to investigate a channeler who claimed she was periodically inhabited by a 10,000-year-old warrior. Consumers, especially older women, were paying up to $5,000 to spend a weekend with this person and listen to the voice of this warrior being channeled through her body. I inquired about coming to one of the sessions and was immediately barraged with calls from her lawyer claiming that her operation was a church and that the state attorney general's office had no authority constitutionally. We dropped the investigation.

The only way law enforcement can address the issue of fake religious organizations is by proving that the operation used the claim of religious affiliation simply as a veil to elude prosecution—and taxes. This has been successfully shown in a number of important cases throughout the United States in recent years.

 "How can I avoid becoming a fraud victim?"

There are three rules of the road which you should remember any time you are making a decision in the marketplace.

1. If it sounds too good to be true, it probably is.

This addresses the sweepstakes mentality. There is no free lunch in the rather ruthless marketplace of the 1990s. You simply need to use common sense and asked yourself, Why is this person willing to offer me such a great deal? The reason may be that he or she wants to rip you off. Don't be afraid to raise the red "fraud alert" flag in your mind.

2. Never make a buying decision at the time of the sales pitch. Always give yourself a voluntary three-day cooling off period.

There is no deal out there in the marketplace that can't wait until you have given yourself time to think it over. If a salesperson is pressuring you to "buy now!" or tells you the offer he or she is making is good only for one day, walk away and don't do business with that person.

Applying pressure to consumers is a classic sales technique that can get even the most sophisticated consumers in trouble. Let me give you an example of my experience with high-pressure sales.

Back in the mid-1980s, camping club promoters were sending notification cards to consumers (especially seniors) stating they had won a prize. The pitch was that they needed to come listen to a ninety-minute sales presentation in order to claim their prize. Most of the time, the prize offered was a cheap barbecue set or a toaster oven.

Once the consumer arrived at the camping club site, he or she would be led on a tour and subsequently into a small room where two or three big salespeople would pressure him or her to buy a membership.

I worked on several cases in which former camping club salespeople testified about how they would sell people on the camping club memberships. They described a technique which we later discovered was used in all kinds of sales environments (including health club membership sales). They would employ what is known as "the drop close."

The salespeople would start by talking about how wonderful the camping facilities they had just toured were and begin to "establish value":

"Now the normal price of a membership at this club is $7,995 and it's worth it, isn't it? I mean we have beautiful grounds, a swimming pool going in next year and everything. But you are in luck today because we have something called the first visit discount. This means that even though the regular price is $7,995, today is your first visit, and if you sign up to become a member today, the membership won't cost you the regular price of $7,995. In fact, it won't even cost you $6,995 or $5,995. No, if you sign up today, the total price for you under the first visit discount is only $4,995. That means if you buy today, you will save a whopping $3,000 off the regular price. Come back tomorrow and the price jumps back up to $7,995. So what are you going to do?"

We asked the former employees of these firms in depositions, "How many camping club memberships did you sell at the so-called regular price of $7,995?" The salespeople just laughed. When we asked them why they were laughing, they told us they didn't sell any at $7,995. One salesperson said, "We just told them the regular price was $7,995 so we could then 'drop' them down to the first visit price and make them think they were saving $3,000. Haven't you guys ever heard of the drop close?"

Up until that time, we hadn't heard of the drop close. This meant of course that the regular price was $4,995 and therefore consumers who thought they were saving $3,000 were in fact not saving a dime.

We reached a point where so many consumers, especially seniors, were complaining that they had been pressured into buying something they didn't really want, that we went to the state legislature and passed a law requiring a three-day cooling off period for the sale of camping clubs. This meant anyone who signed a contract to join a camping club had a three-day period in which he or she could change his or her mind and rescind the contract.

One year after this law went into effect, the owners of the largest camping club in Washington State came to the attorney general's office complaining about the new law. When we asked them what the problem was, they said that 60 percent of the people they had signed up in the past year had exercised their right to cancel within the three-day period.

We told them we thought that meant the law was working. If 60 percent of the people they convinced to sign up changed their minds once they got home and had time to think about it, they must have been pressured into it.

I mention this because there are very few instances under the law where such a mandatory three-day cooling off period exists. But there is no reason why an individual can't simply make it a personal rule to always wait three days after hearing a sales pitch before he or she makes a buying decision.

As was clearly the case with the cost of a camping club membership, there is no deal that can't wait three days to give you time to think it over.

3. Discuss the transaction with someone whose opinion you trust.

So often consumers make decisions in isolation of others whose judgment might prevent problems. For years, we had trouble with insurance salespeople pretending to work for AARP or some other retirement association in order to come into the homes of seniors and sell them unneeded Medigap insurance policies or living trusts. The fact that 31 percent of all seniors live alone lends itself to the isolation tactics of these kinds of salespeople. It is vital that before making a buying decision, you talk to someone whose opinion you trust: your son or daughter, your attorney, the next-door neighbor. Ask their advice and then decide what to do.

Now that you have read a description of a typical question and answer session on the subject of consumer fraud, you should have a clearer sense of the issues on most people's minds.

I want to point out however that reading about such sessions, while hopefully informative, is not a substitute for getting out and going to a meeting. Those who actually get out to the senior center or the AARP chapter meetings or who belong to another group that meets regularly are far less likely to be victimized by the scams you will learn in this book. "United we stand, divided we fall" seems like a cliché, but my experience has been that those who have interaction with others on a regular basis are much less likely to be victimized than those who isolate themselves.

If you don't belong to such a group currently, look up the aging network office in your community or refer to chapter 8 for information about state agencies on aging. Almost every community in the United States has some kind of senior organization which you can join.

CHAPTER 3

THE ABC'S OF FRAUD AGAINST OLDER ADULTS

"Experience teaches us that the man who looks you straight in the eye, particularly if he adds a firm handshake, is hiding something."

—Clifton Fadiman

The best way to arm yourself against fraud is to learn what the basic pitches or approaches sound like in order to be able to quickly identify them. I have put together twenty-six schemes which have been successfully used over and over to target and victimize older adults. The fraud schemes listed in this chapter may be slightly altered by the con artists, who change pitches often, sometimes even daily, to accommodate breaking news stories, changing economic climates, or even their own moods.

As you read through the ABC's of fraud, think about how many of these pitches you have been exposed to in the past or whether you know someone who has been exposed to them. Did the con man or woman use the same exact pitch as it appears here? Is it similar, yet slightly different? Would you be able to identify it as a scam?

Also, think about the people in your community who might benefit from seeing this information. Remember, the mark of a good fraud fighter is not only to protect yourself from fraud, but also to share the knowledge you have with friends, relatives, and neighbors so they too can be protected.

A
ALZHEIMER'S SCHEME

This is perhaps one of the most ruthless schemes out there because it preys on the most vulnerable segment of the senior population: Alzheimer's patients. It begins with a phone call, during which the con artist spends a considerable amount of time talking with the prospective victim. He will ask the person to tell him stories about his or her life. While the victim is talking, the con artist is writing down everything he or she says.

The next day, the con artist will ask the victim questions about stories he or she had mentioned the day before. If the person can't remember the conversation, then the con artist knows that the person's memory is poor. This type of setup leads to the pitch the following day.

THE PITCH

"Joe, Joe this is John. Where is the $25,000 check you agreed to send me? Joe, the oil well investment? What's the matter Joe?"

THE RESULT

A majority of the time the victim will agree to send the money out of embarrassment that he or she may have forgotten a conversation. The con artist is preying on this insecurity and is basically stealing the money since it is a fraudulent oil well investment. However, it is a safe con because if it came down to the con artist's word against that of an elderly person with a failing memory, who do you think would win?

PREVENTION TIP

The best advice for older adults living alone is to never do business over the phone with a stranger. Also, never make a decision to buy at the time of the sales pitch. Always wait at least seventy-two hours and during that time, ask for advice from someone whose opinion you trust.

If you are the caretaker for an Alzheimer's patient or for a senior who simply has declining faculties, make sure that he or she does not write out checks in your absence. The best way to avoid this scheme is to have the victim's finances simplified as much as possible and have a son or daughter or friend whom you trust help the older person.

WHERE TO GO FOR HELP

The local area agency on aging in your community has caseworkers who can help work with older persons with declining mental faculties. The first place to start is with the information and assistance (or referral) number in the phone book. This is a service typically funded by the local area agency on aging and they can provide caseworker referrals and other assistance to older persons.

BANK EXAMINER HOAX

This scheme preys on a senior's desire to help his or her community and on the fear of losing money through bank embezzlement. It starts with a phone call from an official-sounding voice on the other end of the line.

THE PITCH

"Hello, Mrs. Johanson. This is Inspector Joseph Stortelli. I am with the Federal Reserve Bank, special investigations section. It seems that your bank has been having trouble with a dishonest employee exchanging real money with counterfeit and handing it out to its customers.

"Now I am told that you have been a loyal and dedicated customer of the bank for years and that you might be willing to help us catch this person in the act. If you are agreeable, I would like you to go to teller number three tomorrow and withdraw $2,000 in $50 bills. Once you have the money, you can hand it over to me and I will have our investigators inspect the bills to see if they are counterfeit. Then after the inspection, I will personally redeposit the money into your account."

THE RESULT

The customer dutifully goes to the bank to assist in the "investigation." Once the customer has removed the money, it is turned over to the phony investigator who promises to redeposit the money, but who in fact leaves, never to return.

PREVENTION TIP

The first thing to remember is that neither your bank nor any government agency would ever enlist the help of a customer of a bank to conduct an internal investigation. Second, never give out information about your bank account to anyone whom you do not know. In today's age of electronic banking and information systems, having your bank account number may be all that is necessary to remove funds from your account.

Often the targets for the bank examiner scheme will be chosen based on old deposit slips which a senior may have dropped while at the bank. Be careful to hold onto all bank records. Such information can be used by con artists to swindle you.

WHERE TO GO FOR HELP

If this happens to you or to someone you know, you should report it to the local police immediately. The only way you can even attempt to get your money back is by quickly reporting it to the authorities before the con artist has left town.

Since bank examiner con artists are rarely caught, you should do everything you can to avoid falling for this scheme.

CURSE PITCH

This pitch is used by fortune tellers to target older persons who are widowed and are experiencing loneliness and depression. Many times the depression is the result of having recently lost a husband or a friend.

The widow will answer a newspaper ad or other advertisement seeking help for such depression. Sometimes, the victim will be befriended by a fortune teller (who calls herself a "spiritual healer") outside of a store or a senior center. The scheme almost always involves a woman conning another woman.

The fortune teller wants to convince you that your depression is the result of a curse which is causing bad things to happen to you and your family. The root of this curse is based upon money.

THE PITCH

"The person who placed this curse upon your family is powerful in the ways of the dark. The evil is too strong. The only way to debauch yourself from this evil is for you to renounce worldly possessions. It will be difficult, however, I can break the curse. I will fast and pray for three days. At the end of three days, you must bring $4,000 as a sacrifice to show that possessions in this world do not rule you spiritually. We will destroy this money as a testament to the forces of good, as proof that God means more to you than money and belongings."

THE RESULT

The fortune teller is an expert at luring the victim into thinking she is truly cursed and that the only solution is to destroy worldly possessions. The money is delivered three days later, but is not destroyed. The fortune teller acts out a series of ceremonies in which a handkerchief and string are used. After the victim is convinced the ceremony will rid her of the curse, she is given the handkerchief and string and instructed to put the cash in the handkerchief (between $4,000 and $20,000 depending on the size of the curse and the victim's bank account) and tie it with the string and bring it to her.

When the victim delivers the money in the handkerchief, the shrewd con artist makes the switch. Without the victim seeing it, the handkerchief and money are replaced with a bundle of cut paper in a handkerchief that looks just like the one that was handed to her originally.

Your money has been lifted, nothing else. The con artist will probably refuse to take payment for this service, telling you again that money is evil.

PREVENTION TIP

If you are a recently widowed person or are experiencing depression, be extremely cautious of quick-fix advertisements. Never give large quantities of money to anyone, especially when it is to rid you of "evil spirits" or some other impossible-to-document ailment.

The best source of help is your regular physician or therapist. Even if such professionals cannot provide "instant relief" the way some con artists will promise, it is important during periods of emotional vulnerability that you go to reputable medical professionals.

Just like there are no legitimate overnight wealth offers, there are no overnight cures either. Americans spend billions of dollars each year on medical quackery and health fraud schemes. Those over the age of sixty-five represent 60 percent of all heath fraud victims. Don't let yourself become one of them.

WHERE TO GO FOR HELP

The best place to turn if you have been approached with this pitch is to a trusted friend or relative. If the person tells you you mustn't talk to anyone about this, don't believe the scamster—it's just part of the pitch to rip you off.

If you have already been victimized by this "spiritual healer" or some variety thereof, you should report it immediately to your local police department.

DECEPTIVE MEDIGAP INSURANCE POLICY

The sale of Medicare supplement (or Medigap) insurance policies to older adults presents a keen example of a con artist's ability to manipulate his victim.

Insurance agencies set up huge telephone boiler rooms to generate leads for their hundreds of salespeople statewide who are on the street selling Medigap insurance policies. The salespeople call up older adults from a list they purchased from a market research company.

THE PITCH

"Hello, Mrs. Johanson, this is Eileen. I am calling from the Association of Retired Americans. I'm calling because we are going to have a gentleman in your neighborhood tomorrow who will be available to meet with you and explain changes in the law relating to Medicare and the new Catastrophic Care Act. This new law is very complicated and will definitely affect the way you conduct your finances. Are you available to meet at 11:00 A.M.?"

THE RESULT

This pitch was used to give the salesperson a foot in the door. Across the country, salespeople were taking an issue which was at the time being discussed and written about every day in the news media and telling the victims it was going to affect them. The salesperson would convince his victim that his company could help.

Once the appointment was made, the salesperson would come to the older person's home and, instead of talking about Congress and Medicare, would pressure him or her into purchasing insurance policies, whether the person needed them or not.

PREVENTION TIP

Don't be fooled by telemarketers pretending to represent the American Association of Retired Persons (AARP) or some other well-known retirement organization. If you are interested in shopping for a new Medigap insurance policy, let your fingers do the walking in the yellow pages and shop for an insurance agency with a good reputation.

If you have a friend who trusts a particular agent based upon past practices, get that person's name and phone number. Most states have programs offered through the state insurance commissioner's office which assist older persons in deciding which kind of Medigap insurance policy to buy. Call your state insurance commissioner and ask if they have a SHIBA (Senior Health Insurance Benefit Advisor) program or the equivalent.

WHERE TO GO FOR HELP

If you feel you have already been tricked by an insurance agent into buying unnecessary Medigap insurance coverage, contact the consumer division of your state insurance commissioner's office and tell them you would like to file a complaint.

E
EQUITY SKIMMING CON

While door-to-door home improvement schemes have been around for decades, another type of fraud known as equity skimming is relatively new. There are many varieties of this real estate fraud, and most are complicated. They can cost homeowners their homes and their credit ratings.

THE PITCH

One version targets homeowners who are behind in payments and need to sell their homes quickly to avoid foreclosure. The "skimmer" promises to take over the payments and make any back payments for the seller. After the seller has signed over the deed, the skimmer rents out the house, but never assumes the loans or makes any monthly mortgage payments. After some time has passed, foreclosure is begun against the seller.

Another version targets seniors who own their homes free and clear. The con artist approaches a senior who is selling a home and offers to buy the property for the full asking price. However, to close the transaction more quickly and easily, the buyer doesn't go to a bank for financing, but instead proposes a real estate contract. The contract has a clause which says the sale is "subject to a rehabilitation loan" which enables the skimmer to go to a lender and borrow money using the home as collateral.

THE RESULT

After the skimmer has used the house as collateral to borrow thousands of dollars and has possession of the home, he often rents it out. At the same time, the skimmer defaults on the rehabilitation loan and also never makes payments to the seller. Eventually, the seller must take back the house. But in order to do so, he must take over payments on the loan in order to avoid losing it in foreclosure. Meanwhile the skimmer has disappeared with the rehabilitation loan and the rent collected from the house. The senior who started with a house which was owned free and clear now has a house with a new substantial mortgage on it.

PREVENTION TIP

When selling a home, it is critically important to have any contracts or unusual sales arrangements checked out by an attorney. The kind of transaction just described would have been instantly spotted by an objective attorney. In addition, sales should go through normal escrow procedures including the ordering of a title report so that all loan assumptions can be completed before the property changes hands.

WHERE TO GO FOR HELP

If you think this has happened to you, contact your attorney general's office and your attorney immediately.

FREE CAR BAMBOOZLE

This scheme has many variations and can be used on older adults as well as people of other age groups. It preys once again on people's desire to get something for nothing. The targets for this scheme are located from "mooch" lists (previously victimized consumers).

THE PITCH

"Mrs. Green, congratulations. You have just been selected as the grand prize winner! You are going to receive a new, 1993 Cadillac Seville. Have you ever won anything major before? You haven't? Well today is your lucky day. We are going to fly you down here to Las Vegas to be in the winner's circle, you are going to be on TV, the mayor is going to give you the key to the city. Now you don't have to do a thing. My secretary will call you tomorrow with all of the details. Have a great day!"

THE RESULT

The caller hangs up and the victim is so excited that he or she has just won a $25,000 car that the victim starts calling everyone he or she knows. This is exactly what the con artist is hoping for. He wants the "mooch" to become attached to the idea that she has won.

The next day, con artist number two calls. It is the secretary calling back to confirm everything just as promised. She tells the mooch that she is indeed the winner and all she has to do before sending the plane ticket is to take care of the "gift tax." When the mooch says she wasn't told about any gift tax, the con explains that there is a $900 gift tax on the car. The secretary often says, "You do pay your taxes, don't you? You aren't trying to hide anything, are you?" Most of the time, the mooch will pay the $900 in order to avoid losing the $25,000 "free" car.

The con artist then has an overnight express delivery runner go out to the house, pick up the $900 check, run it to the victim's bank, cash it, and that is the last you ever hear of the Cadillac.

PREVENTION TIP

There is no such thing as a free lunch. If someone calls you and tells you you've won, don't believe the person. The best way to get someone to buy something is to tell the person you are giving him or her a free gift, even if you're not! In many states, it is illegal to charge a fee in order to gain the chance to win something. Such an offer is considered an illegal lottery. The best advice when confronted with the "you've won a prize" pitch is to hang up the phone.

WHERE TO GO FOR HELP

If you get a solicitation of this kind, try to find out the name of the company and where it is located and report it to the attorney general's office.

GET RICH QUICK PYRAMID SCHEME

There are literally hundreds of different kinds of pyramid schemes floating throughout the marketplace at any one time. Most claim that for little or no effort, you can "get rich quick" by following a simple set of instructions.

THE PITCH

"This is the opportunity of a lifetime. All you have to do is pay $200 into the plan, recruit five others, and within weeks you will be getting checks for $100 from people all over the country. Hard to believe? I am the biggest skeptic around and I didn't believe it at first either. But you know what made me a believer? $4,400 in cash sent to me in the past ten days. That's $440 per day, every day for the past week and a half. And that's just the beginning. "

THE RESULT
The problem with this type of scheme is that those at the top of the pyramid who started the promotion usually make money. Unfortunately, those who are recruited after several weeks or months and are at the bottom of the pyramid find that there is no one left to recruit. Also, since no material, product, or service is being produced other than perpetuation of the scheme itself, it violates many state's chain distributor schemes laws.

Thus, mere participation in the scheme is enough for those who end up as victims to be sued by attorney general offices.

PREVENTION TIP
You can't get something for nothing in this world no matter how adamant the seller of a pyramid opportunity might be. The best way to avoid falling prey to this kind of a scheme is to ask yourself, Does it sound too good to be true? If the answer is yes, then it is probably a scam and should be avoided at all costs.

WHERE TO GO FOR HELP
Report such offers to the attorney general's office whether or not you have been victimized by a scam of this nature.

HOME REPAIR SWINDLE
This fraud scheme has many variations. The primary approach is to locate a neighborhood where there is a high concentration of seniors. The con artist will prey on fear by telling the senior her roof needs significant repair. He will indicate that he can give her a great deal.

THE PITCH

"Hello ma'am, my name is Frank. I've been working on a job down the street for the past couple of days and as I drove by your house, I couldn't help but notice that you've got some problems with your roof. Now luckily for you, I have some extra material left over from the job I'm finishing down the street and I could do the job for you for just the cost of labor."

THE RESULT

Usually the job is grossly overpriced and the work is either incomplete or shoddily done. These transient roofers will always collect the money up front and then disappear within a few days. Law enforcement finds it nearly impossible to prosecute such con artists since they move around so much.

PREVENTION TIP

Never hire a contractor who has knocked on your door asking for business. Legitimate contractors simply don't do business that way. Also, if you are concerned about the condition of your roof or the siding on your house as a result of such a solicitation, look up three contractors in the yellow pages of the phone book and get competitive bids. Make sure the contractor you hire is licensed and bonded. Always check with the state Department of Labor and Industries or the Department of Licensing to determine if a contractor is licensed and bonded before hiring him.

WHERE TO GO FOR HELP

If you've been taken by one of these home repair "professionals," contact your local attorney general's office.

I'LL FIX YOUR RUSTY BUMPER COME-ON

This scheme involves confronting older adults in parking lots to isolate them and take their money. It preys on gullibility and also the convenience factor of having a chore done without having to take your car into a shop.

THE PITCH

"Hey lady, I can get that rust off your bumper for you in no time. I have this special rust remover solution which instantly transforms the molecular structure of the decaying metal, rejuvenates it, and makes it look like new. Are you interested?"

THE RESULT

The result is that the con artist will charge $75 to $100 to put spray paint over the rust which makes it look better for about a week. He then moves on to the next victim. Since he has no business address and no license, the consumer has no recourse. Also, the victim typically will not tell anyone that this occurred out of embarrassment.

I encountered a guy pitching an older adult in exactly this fashion one summer day in Seattle in a supermarket parking lot. As I was leaving the Elk's lodge in the community of Ballard, I noticed a woman getting into her El Camino. It was an older car with rust all over the rear storage area.

As I watched her get into her car, a guy drove up along side of her and said, "Hey lady, I can get the rust off of the back of your car for ya." To her credit, the woman ignored him and got into her car and left.

The guy who had pitched her saw me staring at him and yelled over, "What are you looking at?" I told him I was from the state attorney general's office and I was just wondering if he had a license to solicit people in supermarket parking lots. He thought for a moment and then said, "Yeah, I got a license—you got a license to wear that suit you're wearin?" The world is just full of comedians. So I said, "Well I'll show you mine, if you'll show me yours!" With that, he sped off.

PREVENTION TIP

Do not do business with people who approach you in unusual places or in unusual ways. If you need services performed on your car, house, or other major personal possessions, the best advice is to let your fingers do the walking in the yellow pages. Get several opinions and then hire the business you believe will give you the best service for the price.

WHERE TO GO FOR HELP

If you fall victim to this kind of scam, call the attorney general's office or your local police.

JUST LET ME TRIM YOUR TREES HORNSWOGGLE

This approach is one of many variations used by con artists who go door to door plying their trade. The danger of hiring such a person is that he is seldom, if ever, licensed and is transient by nature, so it is difficult to find him if problems arise.

THE PITCH

"Well, ma'am, I was in the neighborhood trimming one of your neighbor's trees after that big windstorm we had and I wondered if you would like me to trim your trees . . . some of those big branches look like they could snap off at any moment and fall on your house—you wouldn't want that to happen now would you?"

THE RESULT

This fraud scheme can be handled one of two ways by the con artist. First, he can ask for the money up front, then begin the work and leave, never to return. The result is the victim has paid sometimes as much as several hundred dollars to have a few small limbs trimmed.

The second approach the con artist will use is to start the work by telling the victim that he won't know how much it will cost until he gets "into" the job. On this premise, he will start the work and after cutting down just about every tree in the yard, will hand the victim a bill for $600 to $700! When the victim complains that she did not authorize the work, the con artist threatens to put a workman's lien on the house and foreclose on it if payment is not immediately forthcoming.

PREVENTION TIP

The best thing to remember is that most legitimate contractors do not solicit new business by going door to door. If you are approached in this fashion and are concerned about tree limbs or the condition of a roof or siding, always get three bids from licensed and bonded contractors. Never hire a contractor on the spot who has knocked on your door. Never pay for the job in advance.

The best source for finding legitimate contractors is your local yellow pages directory. You may want to contact your local area agency on aging or information and referral office to find out what chore services are available or if they can recommend particular contractors for routine yard work.

WHERE TO GO FOR HELP

If you have already been taken by an unscrupulous "gardener," report the matter to your local police department or to the state attorney general's office.

KEEP THE PEACE CHARITY SHAM

There are thousands of charitable organizations in every community in America trying to raise money for their causes. The vast majority of these causes are legitimate. Some hire professional fund-raisers from time to time who operate on the border between legal and illegal activity.

The biggest problem with some of these professional fund-raisers is that they keep a majority of the money they raise as their fee and then leave the community from which they raised it. And when it comes to identifying a cause which generates the public's interest, nothing is better than crime.

THE PITCH

"Yes, ma'am, I am calling from the Clarkston Police Department, and you know crime is getting to be a big problem everywhere, even right here in Clarkston—did you see that story about the woman who was attacked last Saturday night while returning from the grocery store?

"The Clarkston Police Guild is an all volunteer organization of police officers who raise money to help support the local police department. You want this community to be safe for our children don't you? I thought so— how about a $100 donation?"

THE RESULT

It may be that the Clarkston police do in fact have a guild and it may be that they do help the department fight crime. The question is how much of any one citizen's $100 contribution actually will go to the guild and how much will go to the telemarketing firm or professional fund-raiser who made the call?

All too often, the fund-raiser cuts a deal with the charity that he will get a certain amount of money and no more. The fund-raiser might even pay the charity the money in advance of raising it. I have seen examples where the fund-raiser gives the charity $5,000 in advance of raising the money. Then the fund-raiser calls citizens from, in this example, the Clarkston Police Guild and gives them the pitch.

The fund-raiser might raise $100,000 for the police guild to fight crime . . . and then leave town. He raised $100,000, but the guild was only promised (and received) $5,000. This means 95 percent of the donations went to the fund-raiser, not the charity.

PREVENTION TIP

Demand to see a breakdown (in writing) of where your contribution dollars are going: how much to the fund-raiser and how much to the charity. Also, make sure the charity is registered with the state to raise money. This usually allows you to check its annual financial reports. Contact the charities division of the secretary of state's office for such information. In addition to contacting the charities department for your state, you can also call your local attorney general's office and find out if there have been any complaints against the firm. You may also call the city in which you live and find out if the firm has a city business or solicitor's license.

WHERE TO GO FOR HELP

If you have given money to a charity and later discovered the money never got to the charity, file a complaint against the fund-raiser with the attorney general's office.

If you are wary about giving to a charity, consider donating to an office drive for such organizations as United Way which have strict rules regarding the amount of your contribution they can spend on overhead costs. You may also consider giving directly to the charity of your choice and bypassing the fund-raiser altogether. This can be done by simply looking up the address of the organization in the phone book and mailing them a check.

What percentage of your donation should go to the fund-raiser versus the charity? Some consumer groups have suggested you use the 80/20 rule as a guideline. That is, for each dollar you contribute, look for organizations which can document that at least 80 percent of that dollar goes to the charitable purpose and no more than 20 percent goes to overhead.

LIVING LEGACY FLIMFLAM

This pitch preys on the almost universal desire to have immortality. For older adults, such immortality is usually achieved through one source: their grandchildren. This pitch preys on the quest for immortality and the emotions that go with it.

THE PITCH

"Now Fred, what I'm talking about here is a living legacy. You know I have a client, Dick Jeffreys. And every month, Dick buys four one-quarter shares. And do you know why? Because he has four grandchildren. And Dick was telling me just the other day, he said, 'Larry, I am so glad that you are in my life now. Because I know that when those kids get those checks after I die, after I'm gone, that they are going to remember their grandfather' . . . and you know Fred, isn't that what it's all about?"

THE RESULT

This pitch is used to sell investments, specifically oil well leases. The investor buys shares at $2,000 to $5,000 each and is promised huge returns, only to find down the road that the oil wells were shallow and rarely, if ever, struck oil. Some con artists will set up a "well site" for $50,000 to $75,000 dollars, then sell up to $1 million worth of investments on it. They will set up the site to avoid criminal prosecution. After all, selling oil leases for nonexistent wells is clearly fraud, selling them on poorly designed, shallow wells is simply deceptive.

PREVENTION TIP

Don't make business decisions based on emotion. The living legacy pitch is clearly an appeal to older persons' emotions for their grandchildren. The best thing you can do for your grandchildren is to invest conservatively and with brokers who are in your own backyard. Never make investments over the phone.

The best "legacy" you can leave to your children and grandchildren is the reputation of being a wise consumer who was not easily fooled by emotional sales pitches and unrealistic profits.

WHERE TO GO FOR HELP

I you feel you have been defrauded or are being harassed by an overzealous broker, report it to the attorney general's office or the National Association of Securities Brokers.

MIRACLE ANTI-AGING FORMULA FRAUD

This pitch is one of many health fraud schemes which targets older adults. It is usually pitched in magazine advertisements which are made to look like news stories. This grabs the reader's attention and explains in part why the product can do things which modern medicine simply could never do before. By making the ad look like a news story, the reader tends to believe it.

THE PITCH

> ### New Anti-Aging Formula Uncovered After Fall of Iron Curtain . . .
>
> The fall of the Berlin Wall has freed more than just those in Eastern Europe. It has made available for the first time outside of the iron curtain an anti-aging formula so powerful that physicians everywhere are calling it the "Fountain of Youth." Studies released from experiments done in East Germany claim that patients who have used this new miracle formula have increased their life expectancy by as much as thirty years!

THE RESULT

So what is this new anti-aging miracle formula? Normal strength vitamins which you could purchase at any grocery store for one-fourth the price. The older person is duped into thinking he or she can add thirty years onto his or her life, so is willing to pay a premium price for it.

How do I know that this product was nothing more than vitamins? I called the number listed in this advertisement last year. I asked about the new anti-aging formula just released because of the fall of the Berlin Wall. The person who answered the phone said, "What are you talking about—we sell vitamins." I then said, "But I was sent an advertisement with your phone number on it which claims you have a miracle anti-aging formula." The woman on the other end of the phone paused for a moment and then said, "Oh the anti-aging formula . . . sure we sell that. How many boxes do you want?"

PREVENTION TIP

Medical quackery is big business and most of it targets older adults. The simple way to avoid it is by consulting your regular physician any time you read about or are solicited to purchase over-the-counter medicine or vitamins which promise extraordinary results.

This advice is especially important if you have purchased vitamins or other types of drugs through the mail and the instructions advise you to stop taking your physician-prescribed drugs. Such stoppage can lead to severe consequences.

WHERE TO GO FOR HELP

Your own personal physician is the best source of advice on medical matters. If you have a complaint about your doctor, contact the state medical disciplinary board in your state.

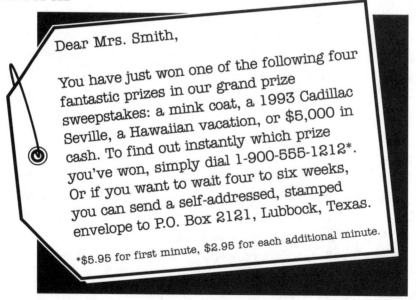

900 NUMBER CHICANERY

This scam is new in the marketplace. It preys on the confusion consumers have with the difference between "800" toll-free numbers and "900" numbers which always result in a toll charge. A survey of the older consumer conducted by the Pennsylvania Attorney General's office recently indicated that 45 percent of those surveyed didn't know the difference between a 900 and an 800 number.

Sometimes the charge can be as much as $10 per minute. How do they get you to call the number? Either through a direct mail flyer or an ad in newspapers.

THE PITCH

Dear Mrs. Smith,

You have just won one of the following four fantastic prizes in our grand prize sweepstakes: a mink coat, a 1993 Cadillac Seville, a Hawaiian vacation, or $5,000 in cash. To find out instantly which prize you've won, simply dial 1-900-555-1212*. Or if you want to wait four to six weeks, you can send a self-addressed, stamped envelope to P.O. Box 2121, Lubbock, Texas.

*$5.95 for first minute, $2.95 for each additional minute.

THE RESULT

The consumer is induced to dial the 900 number because of the prospect of winning the new Cadillac or $5,000 in cash. The letter is written such that it complies with most states' gambling/lottery statutes.

Once the consumer calls, he or she is either put on hold (which increases the eventual bill) or is told he or she has won the Hawaiian trip. This trip usually turns out to be for accommodations only and the consumer must fly there at his or her own expense.

The phone bill which the consumer receives at the end of the month will include a charge which could be as high as $60, depending on the rates and the duration of the call. The con artist gets most of this money since the phone company deducts its normal charges and then passes the rest on to its client who leased the 900 service.

With a variation on this scam the customer calls an 800 "toll-free" number and is instructed to press a number, which switches him or her to a 900 number. This should be reported to the phone company and the attorney general's office immediately.

PREVENTION TIP

There are many legitimate uses of 900 numbers such as conducting polls, and collecting research information. But if you see a solicitation telling you that you have won an incredible prize, don't fall for it. The chances are you are being told that just so you call the 900 number.

WHERE TO GO FOR HELP

If you find a 900 number charge on your phone bill that you didn't authorize or that you dispute, the next step is to contact your phone company and request that the charge be removed. If this doesn't work, call the attorney general's office and file a complaint against the 900 company.

OBITUARY FARCE

This scheme is so cruel it seems impossible that a con artist or anyone else for that matter would stoop so low. It preys on widows and widowers by pretending to deliver a Bible ordered by the deceased spouse. The con artist literally looks in the obituary column of the local newspaper to learn information about the deceased, including names of the surviving family.

Then with a minor amount of detective work, the surviving spouse's address and phone number are located.

THE PITCH

"Mrs. Robertson, my name is Frank Anderson. I represent the American Bible Company. Two weeks ago, your husband placed an order for our deluxe edition of the King James Bible. He asked that the gold inlay inscription be made out to 'Dolores Robertson'. Why that must be you. He must have meant this as a gift for you."

THE RESULT

The typical result is the surviving spouse will purchase the Bible at a grossly inflated cost (supposedly due to the gold-inlay inscription) and no one is the wiser.

The danger of falling for this pitch goes beyond the $80 to $100 the victim might spend on the Bible. Once the con artist network has identified a vulnerable target, the victim will be contacted over and over again by other charlatans seeking to con her.

PREVENTION TIP

Con artists use obituary columns as a source of leads to sell other products besides Bibles. Because survivors are distraught and vulnerable, it is not uncommon for insurance salespeople, investment brokers, or Realtors to call on the bereaved survivor.

Individuals who have experienced the loss of a loved one should make a personal rule to avoid nonessential buying decisions for a minimum of six months! This will give them time to stabilize from the trauma of losing a spouse or loved one and will provide protection from con artists seeking to exploit such grief.

WHERE TO GO FOR HELP

If you know someone who you feel might be vulnerable to this kind of pitch due to recently losing a loved one, call your local information and area agency on aging and ask about the senior companion program and other programs which can help alleviate loneliness and depression.

PIGEON DROP, CLASSIC DOUBLE-DEALING

The pigeon drop is one of the oldest and, unfortunately, most reliable fraud schemes around. And the vast majority of victims are seniors.

The scam involves two con artists of either sex working together, but who pretend to be strangers. The first one will approach a senior and strike up a conversation. While doing so, he will plant a bag nearby which has cut paper wrapped in $20 or $50 bills in it to appear like a vast sum of money. Then con artist number two comes along.

THE PITCH

"Excuse me ma'am—is that your bag sitting there? It isn't? I wonder whose it is (the schemer looks inside). Oh my gosh–there must be $5,000 in here!"

The schemer looks to his accomplice.

"Is this yours, young lady? It isn't, well what are we going to do? You know, I have heard of this happening before because my father is a police lieutenant. I'm going to go call him."

The schemer leaves, then returns after five minutes.

"My dad said it's finders keepers if no one claims it in a week. He said he'll hold it for us down at the station, but we need to put up a $500 bond. If no one claims it in a week, the three of us get to split $5,000!"

THE RESULT

The victim is excited about the prospect of splitting this large sum of money and decides to trust the two strangers, especially the man who claims to be the son of a police officer. She agrees to put up the $500 bond money in order to have a chance at splitting the $5,000. She goes to her bank accompanied by the two con artists, withdraws the money and then gives it to the "policeman's son" so he can take it down to the station. The con artist might even give the victim the (phoney) name of his father so that she can ask for him one week hence.

After a week has passed, the victim goes down to the police station and finds no one by that name working there, no $500 bond money, and no $5,000 in lost money.

PREVENTION TIP

The best way to avoid this scam is to report any lost money directly to the police and try not to let greed tempt you into making an unwise decision. Never enter into a business relationship with someone whom you do not know no matter what that person tells you.

WHERE TO GO FOR HELP

If you have been defrauded in this way, report it to the police and the attorney general's office immediately.

QUACKERY ILLUSION

Seniors account for 12 percent of the U.S. population, yet they are 60 percent of the victims of health fraud and medical quackery. While there are numerous examples of such quackery, a time-tested pitch preys on victims of arthritis. Tabloid magazines are full of print advertisements which claim to have found some new miracle cure.

THE PITCH

MIRACLE CURE!

Thousands of cancer patients from Australia are raving about a new cancer treatment which utilizes an iodized water solution to treat advanced cancer patients. Case studies which have been reported claim the solution has lead to instantaneous remission in hundreds of scientifically documented cases.

Criticized by the American medical community as a fad and "risky," Australian doctors and their patients have proclaimed the new treatment "a miracle" and "the answer to our prayers." The Australian press has cited story after story of grateful patients who had lost all hope until trying the miracle treatment.

For more information about this incredible discovery, send $29.95 to: Cancer Treatment Center, P.O. Box 4422, New York, New York 20013.

THE RESULT

All too often the victim, who may be in excruciating pain and who has gotten little substantive relief from the "American medical community," is willing to send away for this miracle cure.

In some cases, the person receives nothing in return and finds, upon investigation, that he or she has sent money to a post office box which was closed one week after it was mailed in.

In more serious cases, the arthritis sufferer may be sent some kind of pills or liquid solution with instructions to stop taking other medication and take the "new wonder drug." This "new wonder drug" might very well have been produced by con artists with no medical knowledge or background. Ingestion without your physician's approval might prove to be very dangerous, if not fatal.

PREVENTION TIP

It is inadvisable not to take any drugs without the express consent of your regular physician. In this age of rapid medical advancement, it is unlikely that any true breakthroughs in the treatment of cancer or arthritis would be reported by a tabloid magazine or a private entrepreneur advertising in a tabloid. If you are interested in determining if a new drug has been licensed for use in the U.S., call your physician or the Food and Drug Administration office in your community.

WHERE TO GO FOR HELP

If you discover you have been duped by a miracle health formula or similar product, contact your local attorney general's office.

RARE COIN DECEPTION

This scam is very clever and relies on the fact that there are very few regulations or standards for the sale of coins in the United States. Of particular concern is the lack of standards in the grading of coins, the establishment of the "mint state" (MS) of a particular coin.

Because there are several different grading services in the United States, it is possible for telemarketers to pay liberal graders of coins a set fee and have their coins which should come back as an MS 60 be certified as an MS 64. The difference between these MS levels can be several thousand dollars depending on the coin. The consumer is sent the coin with a written appraisal of the mint state and, once he or she sees it, will place the coin or coins in a safety deposit box.

The discrepancy between real and stated MS levels may not be discovered for years while the coins sit tucked away in the victim's safety deposit box.

THE PITCH

"Gladys, you know that all is not well with the world today. There is fighting in the Middle East, the banks are failing, the S&L crisis threatens the solvency of the federal government. In unstable times like these precious metals represent real value you can hold onto when everything else involves uncertainty.

"I have just received a beautiful set of Morgan silver dollars back from the appraiser and they were graded at MS 64. These are fine quality coins which are going to do nothing but go up, up, up in value. I am going to ship five of them off to you today, OK?"

THE RESULT

Once again, Gladys might very well receive her Morgan silver dollars and the official grading documents, place them in a safety deposit box, and never take them out until she moves. In the meantime, the company that sold them may have paid $125 each for them on the basis that their true MS was 60, then sold them to Gladys for $500 each, claiming they were MS 64's.

PREVENTION TIP

Never buy rare coins over the telephone. It is a complex investment and it is important to know what you're doing. It is also very important to investigate the grading service which grades the coins. There are several which most traders in the industry acknowledge to grade one or two levels higher than they should. This can have an enormous effect on the price. To determine whether a coin has been graded properly, contact a reputable dealer who has been in business in your community for years.

WHERE TO GO FOR HELP

If you feel you have been ripped off by someone who sold you overvalued coins, you should first send a registered letter to the firm demanding a refund. If that fails, contact the attorney general's office in your state and file a complaint.

SPECIAL THIS WEEK
RUG CLEANER HOODWINK

This scam is one of many forms of bait and switch. The general concept is to offer an unbelievably low price in print advertising or in a telephone pitch, then bump up the price once in the home.

THE PITCH

"Hello, Mrs. Carlson, this is Joyce from American Home Cleaning services. We are having a special in your neighborhood this week. We can clean any size living room, dining room, or hallway carpet for the incredibly low price of $14.95. Are you interested in scheduling an appointment?"

THE RESULT

The consumer agrees to let the company come out to the home to clean the carpet for $14.95. However, as soon as the company representative arrives, he or she begins to upsell. "These are much larger rooms than normal, we'll have to charge additional for them. Also, you need carpet protector for this heavy traffic area."

The salesperson usually leaves with a check for $60 to $80. And that was his or her intention all along. In the mid-1980s, I handled several cases where ex-employees testified that they were instructed to upsell the customer a minimum of 100 percent above the originally quoted price.

Several of these employees were fired because they refused to do this. In other words, the company said, "If you don't double the bill once in the home, you're fired." This is textbook institutionalized bait and switch.

PREVENTION TIP

This kind of practice continues today throughout the United States. If you are quoted what seems like an impossibly low price over the phone, either ignore the offer or if you want to look into it more, make the company stick to its promise. If it refuses to do the job for the originally quoted price, then kick the salesperson out of your house.

WHERE TO GO FOR HELP

If you feel you have been "bated and switched" you should report the company to the attorney general's office.

TRANSFER TO A LIVING TRUST DUPE

A living trust is not in itself fraudulent. There are some companies that are aggressively marketing living trusts and representing that they are an essential estate planning tool for everyone.

These sales presentations often take place in settings where older adults are meeting anyway: senior centers, retired teacher meetings, retired teamsters meetings, or special meetings set up to inform seniors about estate planning. The primary method of selling is to scare older adults by reciting horror stories of individuals who have lost up to 90 percent of their estates via the costs of probate.

THE PITCH

"Hello, is this Mrs. Jones? Did you know probate can cost you up to 90 percent of the value of your estate? I've seen it happen over and over: lawyers charging a fixed percentage of the value of your estate, regardless of how much work they do, inheritance tax whittling away at your estate, not to mention the threat of lawsuits by unhappy relatives who feel they should have been included in the will. Now you can avoid the 'agony of probate' and all of these costs by signing a living trust."

THE RESULT

These salespersons claim that by buying a living trust which costs between $900 and $4,000, you can avoid probate and save thousands of dollars. The problem is that the probate laws vary greatly from state to state and many of these firms are using the same scare tactics in multiple states, paying little attention to the differences in laws from one state to the next.

In many states, the probate process has been streamlined so that estates can be probated for less than the fee of several thousand dollars some firms charge.

PREVENTION TIP

The living trust can be an effective estate planning tool for some people. The best way to avoid problems with the probate process and living trusts is to get independent legal advice from an attorney whose opinion you trust. The simple question to ask your attorney is, "Will executing a living trust save me or my family money?" If the answer is no, then don't buy one.

WHERE TO GO FOR HELP

If you have difficulty with living trusts, contact your attorney or the attorney general's office.

UNCLAIMED PROPERTY TRICK

The unclaimed property pitch is based on laws in almost every state which call for unclaimed or abandoned property to revert to the state general fund after a certain period of time.

In many states, for example, if one's mother died leaving a savings account unclaimed (not listed in the will), the money in that account would be transferred to the state department of revenue and added to the unclaimed property rolls.

Because such unclaimed property rolls are public record, entrepreneurs can access this information, record the names on the list, record the amount of the unclaimed asset, and then contact the relative by mail.

THE PITCH

Dear Mrs. Jones:

This letter is to inform you that you have a significant unclaimed asset being held for you. This asset formerly belonged to a legal relative of yours who has subsequently passed away and abandoned the asset.

To claim this asset, please fill out the enclosed application form and remit within thirty days to the address listed below.

THE RESULT
You submit the application that calls for you to sign a contract which allows the firm that contacted you to keep 33 to 50 percent of the asset as its fee for locating the unclaimed property and notifying you of its whereabouts.

PREVENTION TIP
Normally a simple phone call will enable you to determine if your relative is listed on that state's unclaimed property rolls and what you have to do to claim the property.

Many states have limits on how much such "asset locator" firms can charge. In Washington State for example, the limit is 5 percent of the asset's value. Remember though, if you can find it yourself, you are under no obligation to pay anyone a fee. If you are having trouble locating unclaimed property which you feel might be rightfully yours, you should contact family members and brainstorm whose asset it is and which state it might be located in.

WHERE TO GO FOR HELP

If you have already done business with such an unclaimed property "locator" and feel you were overcharged, you can file a complaint with your attorney general's office against the firm. If the company was a law firm, you can still file a complaint against them with the state attorney general's office because it is a dispute over fees, not quality of legal services. Complaints about quality of legal services are generally handled by the state bar association.

VITAMINS SCAM

The vitamins scam preys on seniors because they are very health-conscious and are always looking for savings on drugs of any kind. And because they are on a fixed income, older adults tend to be concerned about finances which makes the idea of "winning" particularly attractive.

THE PITCH

"Congratulations, Mrs. Olson! You have been selected as the winner of one of the following four fabulous prizes: a trip to Europe, $5,000 in cash, a brand new stereo, or a diamond necklace worth $3,000. Now in order to find out which prize you have won, all you have to do is participate in a special promotion. Today only, we are offering a 50 percent discount on our popular Health-Wise vitamin products. Today only we are offering a thirty-day supply for $500 below the regular price of $999."

THE RESULT

The result is that the older adult is enticed by the prospect of winning the prize and is convinced that the vitamins are a good deal, so she orders them. When they arrive, the victim notices that the vitamins she bought were grossly overpriced compared to what she could have purchased them for in a grocery store. The consumer also realizes the prize she won, the diamond necklace supposedly worth $3,000, is a cheap plastic travel case with a retail value of under $20.

This so-called "one of four" promotions has been used by telemarketing fraud boiler rooms for years and is still very much being used today.

PREVENTION TIP

The best thing to remember is that you can't get something for nothing—ever. Don't fall victim to the sweepstakes mentality even if a telemarketer calls and says you've won. No legitimate business is in business to give away expensive prizes.

WHERE TO GO FOR HELP

If you have been taken by the vitamins scam, the first thing to do is notify the firm in writing that you want a complete refund. Believe it or not, many of these fraud rooms offer thirty-day money back guarantees in order to avoid the heat from law enforcement. If this fails, you should contact your local attorney general's office.

W
WORK AT HOME OPPORTUNITY

This scam is time-tested and preys on the consumer's desire to earn money in the privacy of his or her own home. Like so many other scams, it also exploits the "something for nothing" mentality. The pitch usually comes in the form of an ad in the classified section of many magazines and newspapers. The grocery store tabloids are a prime vehicle for this kind of scam.

THE PITCH

> **EARN UP TO $1,000 PER WEEK IN THE PRIVACY OF YOUR OWN HOME STUFFING ENVELOPES.**
> For more information, send $5.00 and a self-addressed stamped envelope to:
> P.O. Box 1113, Miami, Florida.

THE RESULT

Many of these ads are straight frauds, where you receive nothing in return. In those cases where you do get something in return, it is usually instructions to place an ad in the newspaper like the one you responded to, telling others how they can earn thousands per week stuffing envelopes if they send you $5.00. The way you earn $1,000 per week is by perpetuating the scheme. There is no company willing to pay a dollar per envelope, for example.

A recent twist on this pitch is to offer the same opportunity for no fee. The catch is you send a self-addressed, stamped envelope, only to have the con artist send you back a response saying to really get the information, you must send in the $5.00. This approach is designed to elude law enforcement and to psychologically hook the person into following through.

PREVENTION TIP

In today's automated world, it is inconceivable that anyone would hire individuals to stuff envelopes when machines can stuff thousands of envelopes in a short period of time. Do not be fooled by such claims. They are simply all fraud schemes.

How do I know older adults are targeted for this scheme? The next time you go to the grocery store, look in the back of any tabloid magazine under "money-making opportunities." The vast majority of ads listed are work at home schemes of one kind or another.

One day, I went into the grocery store and bought every tabloid they had to research this issue. That was all I bought—five tabloid magazines.

As the clerk was ringing up the magazines, I said, "Aren't you going to ask me why I'm buying these?" She looked up at me and without hesitation said, "It's simple, you're going to grandma's house." Legitimate jobs are listed in the help wanted section of your local newspaper.

WHERE TO GO FOR HELP

It is important to realize that once you send your money in along with your name (and often your phone number), con artists then consider you to be a prime target for a variety of other scams. Therefore, if you have fallen for this pitch or a similar one, report it to the attorney general's office. It may be only $5.00, but the act of filing a complaint is empowering in and of itself and should help you avoid falling for other scams.

XENOPHOBIA SCHEME

This pitch exploits the fear of becoming the victim of crime at the hands of a stranger. The con artist's goal is to convince the victim that he is a police officer whose only interest is protecting the victim from evil criminals. The initial approach is usually done by knocking on the target's door.

THE PITCH

"Mrs. Jones, this is Detective Johnson from the police department (shows badge). We caught a prowler in your alley last night and his accomplice got away. We think he might come back to rob you. So what I would like to do is mark all of your valuables so we can trace them if they are stolen."

THE RESULT

The victim lets the con artist in, then begins to bring out all of her valuables such as cash, antiques, and jewelry so the "officer" can mark them. Once the victim's valuables have been identified, the con artist explains that he left his marking device back at the station. He suggests that for the convenience of the victim, he is willing to inventory the valuables, give the victim a police receipt, and then take the items down to the station to be marked. He promises to return them within one hour. He then leaves never to return.

PREVENTION TIP

If someone knocks on your door or calls you on the phone claiming to be a law enforcement official, make sure you get the badge number and independently call the police station to verify the person's identity. And if he or she asks to see your valuables, don't do it! There is no circumstance where a police officer would want to take possession of money and jewelry for prevention purposes.

Many local police departments do offer to loan marking devices for purposes of engraving your driver's license number on valuables. This activity, when combined with displaying an "operation identification" sticker on a window of your home, can be an effective deterrent to burglars who have a difficult time fencing marked property.

It is important to cooperate with the local police department if you are contacted. But it is more important to protect yourself from clever con artists by verifying the identity of the person before dealing with him or her.

If you have taken positive steps to avoid being burglarized like joining neighborhood watch and securing locks on doors and windows, you should rest easy. Contact your local police department for more information.

WHERE TO GO FOR HELP

If you have been approached in this fashion and handed over valuables to a stranger, it is important to call the police immediately and report the swindle. The speed with which you report this type of crime is of crucial importance in increasing your chances of getting the valuables back.

YOU DENTED MY CAR ACT

This scheme is one of a variety of pitches which confront older adults in parking lots. It preys on the insecurity many older adults have about driving. The con artist is looking for an older person who pulls into a grocery store parking lot during the middle of the day. He chooses this time because he knows that is when many seniors like to shop in order to avoid crowds. The absence of crowds also helps him pull off his scheme.

The con artist will wait until the senior has gotten out of his car, then the schemer will pull up along side of it in his car which has a dent in the side. He will park his car close to that of the target so that his pitch will be more believable. When the senior returns from shopping, he gets pitched.

THE PITCH

"Hey, is this your car mister? It is? Well look what you did when you pulled in here. I have a huge dent in the side of my car. Some guy told me he saw the whole thing and before he left he gave me his name and phone number. Now I think we can settle this without involving our insurance companies. I don't know about you, but my premiums are high enough as it is."

THE RESULT

The con artist claims he just had that fender repaired and it cost him $547. He offers to drop the whole thing and not tell the victim's insurance company for $250 in cash. Often the senior will fall for it out of insecurity about his driving and out of fear that his insurance company will drop him if he has a claim at his age.

PREVENTION TIP

The first thing to remember is to have self-confidence in your abilities. Do not let anyone intimidate you. Secondly, if confronted in this way, the best thing to do is to insist that the police come to fill out a report. This serves two purposes: first, if you did hit the person's car, driving off might result in an allegation of "hit and run." More importantly, if it is a con game, any mention of the police will scare the con artist away.

If you live in a larger city, you may want to look into taking the bus to the store. Your local metro should be able to give you schedule information.

WHERE TO GO FOR HELP

If you think you have been taken in this fashion by a con artist, report it to the police immediately. Once again, the speed with which you report such an incident and the extent to which you can describe the con artist will largely determine your chances of getting your money returned.

ZIRCONIUM NECKLACE IMPOSTOR

This pitch, like so many others, preys on the "sweepstakes mentality," the mistaken belief that it is possible to get something for nothing, or at least something for very little.

THE PITCH

"Mrs. Brown, congratulations! You have just won a stunning two-carat zirconium necklace with a fourteen-carat gold chain and original design setting. This exquisite treasure normally retails for well in excess of $250. All we need from you is a nominal fee for mounting and we can ship this lovely gem off to you in today's mail!"

THE RESULT

The zirconium jewelry usually looks more like a ball of glue than an "exquisite treasure." The "nominal fee" that one must pay is typically $24.95 and the necklace itself might be worth $6 to $8 at the most. The con artist is indeed delivering a product so as to avoid criminal prosecution, but is grossly inflating the value of the product which the consumer has supposedly "won."

PREVENTION TIP

Once again, you cannot get something for nothing in the rough and tumble world of trade and commerce in America (or any country for that matter). The best thing to do when confronted with a telephone call or direct mail solicitation claiming you have won something is to hang up the phone or throw the solicitation in the trash.

WHERE TO GO FOR HELP

Report any such solicitation to the attorney general's office and file a complaint if you have been victimized.

Remember that many such offers have a twofold purpose: to take your $25 and identify you as a prime "mooch" or sucker who can be recontacted and taken over and over and over. Don't let that happen to you.

THE ABC'S OF FRAUD

THE PITCH	THE RESULT	PREVENTION TIP	WHERE TO GET HELP
Alzheimer's Scheme: "Joe? This is John. Where is the $25,000 check you agreed to send me? Joe? What's the matter Joe?"	The victim agrees to send money out of fear of being embarrassed that he or she forgot the conversation.	If you know someone who may have Alzheimer's, get a son or daughter to cosign all checks. Insist that the person never buy anything over the phone.	If you have been swindled or know someone who may have been, contact your local attorney general's office.
Bank Examiner Hoax: "Ma'am, we'd like you to help us catch a dishonest bank employee by withdrawing $2,000 from your account."	Victim goes to bank, withdraws the money, gives it to phony bank examiner, and never sees it again.	No bank asks customers to help investigate embezzlement. Never give a stranger cash.	If you have given money to someone claiming to be a bank examiner, report it immediately to the police.
Curse Pitch: "There is a curse on your family. The only way to get rid of it is to bring me earthly possessions like $4,000 in cash. We'll destroy the cash as your testament to the forces of good, thereby breaking the curse."	You bring the cash and after performing some impressive ceremonies, the fortune tellers make it look like the money has been destroyed. In fact, by slight of hand, they have switched the cash with cut paper. They burn the paper and you think the curse has been removed.	Don't be fooled by this. If you have spiritual issues you need to address, consult with your local church or parish.	If you have been taken in this fashion, contact the police immediately.
Deceptive Medigap Insurance Policy: "We want to come to your home and discuss our retirement association benefits and what Congress is doing to social security."	Once in your home, the salesperson delivers a high-pressure sales pitch about Medigap insurance.	Never let a salesperson come to your home. Always go to his place of business and give yourself three days to think it over.	If you have been approached in this fashion, call the state insurance commissioner's office and file a complaint.
Equity Skimming Con: "I'd like to buy your house for the full asking price. I have all the paper work right here—just sign on the dotted line."	The con artist will get you to sign a real estate contract that gives him the ability to take out an equity loan on your home and run away without paying.	Never sign legal documents without having an attorney review them first.	If you think this has happened to you, contact your local attorney general's office.
Free Car Bamboozle: "Congratulations! You've just won a new car! All you have to do is pay the gift tax and we'll send you your grand prize."	The "gift tax" is really a gift to the con artist who will send an overnight carrier to your home to pick up your check, never to be seen again.	Never do business with anyone who says you have won a prize—period!!	If you get a solicitation of this kind, try to get the name of the company and where it is located and report it to the attorney general's office.

The Pitch	What It Really Is	What To Do
Get Rich Quick Pyramid Scheme: "This is an opportunity of a lifetime. All you have to do is pay $200 and then recruit five other people and you will receive $100 a week for life!"	This is a pyramid scheme which makes money for those who start the scam, but not for anyone else.	You can't get something for nothing. Don't get involved in any kind of pyramid scheme.	Report such offers to the attorney general's office whether or not you have been victimized.
Home Repair Swindle: "I was doing a job down the street and I noticed your roof looks bad. I could give you a great deal on repairing it."	The con artist requires payment in advance and does only part of the job, then leaves, never to return.	Never hire a door-to-door contractor even if you need the work done. Look for contractors in the yellow pages.	Always check with the state Dept. of Labor and Industries or the Dept. of Licensing to determine if a contractor is licensed and bonded.
I'll Fix Your Bumper Come-On: "I can get the rust off of that bumper for you for a really low price. It'll only take a few minutes."	The con artist will charge between $50 and $150 to put spray paint on your car, which rusts through within weeks.	Don't fall for pitches from people who approach you on the street. Do business with established shops.	If you fall victim to this kind of a scam, call the attorney general's office.
Just Let Me Trim Your Trees Hornswoggle: "I was in the neighborhood doing a lawn job and I have some extra time to trim your hedges."	Often the con artist will ask for the money in advance, trim a few branches, and then flee without completing the job.	Never hire a contractor who has knocked on your door, no matter how innocent he seems. Consult your yellow pages for names of gardeners or yard work professionals.	Call the local police or your attorney general's office if you have been taken.
Keep the Peace Charity Sham: "I'm calling from the local police department and would like a donation to help fight crime in your neighborhood."	The "fund-raiser" will pocket most of the money, and very little will go to the actual charity. The fund-raiser will then leave town.	Demand to see a breakdown (in writing) of where your contribution dollars are going. Make sure the charity is registered with the state to raise money.	If you have given money to a charity, but the money never got there, file a complaint against the fund-raiser with the local attorney general's office.
Living Legacy Flimflam: "What we're talking about here is a living legacy. One of my clients buys investment shares for his grandkids. He likes it because his grandkids will remember him."	This pitch can be used to sell any kind of investment. It preys on emotionalism and an older person's love for his grandkids.	Never buy based on emotional appeals. Give yourself a three-day cooling off period before you make a buying decision.	If you feel you have been defrauded, report it to the attorney general's office.
Miracle Anti-Aging Formula Fraud: "The fall of the Berlin Wall has revealed a new anti-aging formula that can take as much as twenty years off of your life."	This "miracle" is really nothing more than vitamins which you pay as much as 400 percent more for than in a store.	Don't be tempted by medical quackery. Always consult your physician before taking any medication.	If you have a complaint about a particular drug you have purchased, check with your doctor or the Food and Drug Administration.

THE ABC'S OF FRAUD

THE PITCH	THE RESULT	PREVENTION TIP	WHERE TO GET HELP
900 Number Chicanery: "You have just won one of four fabulous prizes! Just call this 900 number to find out what you have won."	The 900 number is a toll charge that could cost you as much as $50. The prize is often a cheap zirconium necklace worth $2 to $3.	Resist any pitch that involves a free prize. They are almost all cons.	If you've fallen for this scam, contact the phone company and ask them to remove the charge. If this doesn't work, file a complaint with the attorney general's office.
Obituary Farce: "Your spouse ordered this gold-inlay Bible for you. He/she thought you would be very pleased with its high quality."	The con artist has gotten your name from the obituary column. He knows your spouse has died and is preying on your sympathies.	Don't buy anything based on emotions. This is a common ploy among con artists.	Contact the police if you have been the victim of this scam or if you know someone who has fallen for it.
Pigeon Drop: "I just found this bag lying here and it is full of cash. We need to leave it at the police station, and I'll split it with you if you give me $500 in bond money."	The con artist is banking on your greediness and dishonesty. You give him the "bond money," but the money is never taken to the police station. The crooks run off with it.	Be distrustful of anyone who approaches you on the street with an opportunity to get rich quick. It just won't happen.	If you have been defrauded in this way, report it to the police or to the attorney general's office.
Quackery Illusion: "A new miracle cure for cancer has been discovered by Australian scientists. Send $29.95 for more information."	You may be desperate enough to send away for such an offer, only to receive a medication which may be ineffective at best and dangerous at worst.	Always consult your physician before trying alternate treatments of any kind.	If you are worried about a drug you have taken, contact the Food and Drug Administration office in your community to find out if it has been licensed for use in the United States.
Rare Coin Deception: "In these troubled times silver is the one investment you can count on. We have a great deal on Morgan silver dollars which will double in value in two years."	Rare coin investments are a complicated investment and should never be done over the phone. You may end up paying double the actual value.	Deal only with local, legitimate dealers.	If you are concerned about the value of coins you purchased, contact a reputable dealer who has been in business in your community for years. Report any scams to the police and the local attorney general's office.
Special This Week Rug Cleaner Hoodwink: "We have a special this week: we'll clean any living room, dining room, and hallway carpet for the low price of $14.95."	The cleaner will often quote you a low price to get his or her foot in the door, then jack the price up to reflect the true price.	Be skeptical of such pitches. If you decide to hire such a firm, insist on paying only the price quoted over the phone.	If you feel you have been "baited and switched," you should report the company to the attorney general's office.

Scam	Reality	What to Do
Transfer to a Living Trust Dupe: "Your children could lose up to 90 percent of their inheritance to greedy lawyers due to the 'agony of probate'. Buy a living trust and avoid probate altogether."	Living trusts are useful for some, but not for all. Many states have streamlined probate systems which are cheap and preclude the need for a living trust.	Check with your own attorney or an accountant to determine if you could benefit from a living trust.	If you have difficulties with living trusts, contact your attorney or the attorney general's office.
Unclaimed Property Trick: "A relative has left you an asset which is waiting to be claimed. This law firm specializes in unclaimed property. To claim your asset, sign the enclosed form and return it forthwith."	The form you sign authorizes the law firm or another party to keep as much as 50 percent of the unclaimed property left by your relative.	If you can trace the relative to a particular state, call the department of revenue, unclaimed property division, and ask if there is an asset listed. There is no charge if you do it that way.	If you are having trouble locating unclaimed property which you feel might be yours, you should contact family members and brainstorm whose asset it is and in which state it might be located.
Vitamins Scam: "You've won one of four fabulous prizes worth thousands of dollars. All you have to do is buy $999 worth of vitamins at our sale price of $500 and we'll tell you what you've won."	The vitamins are worth about $50 and the prize you win is usually an inexpensive cubic zirconium necklace worth about $10.	The free prize pitch should be your clue to hang up the phone no matter how tempting the offer sounds.	If you have fallen for this, contact the attorney general's office immediately and file a complaint.
Work at Home Opportunity: "Earn up to $1,000 per week stuffing envelopes in the privacy of your own home. Send $10 to find out how."	These are all scams. Send in $10 and they send back instructions asking you to put an ad in the paper just like the one you responded to so others will send you $10 to find out how to earn $1,000.	If it sounds too good to be true, it isn't true. No company is going to pay you $1 to stuff an envelope when machines can do it much quicker and cheaper.	Legitimate job offers are listed in the help wanted section of your local newspaper. If you have been taken by this type of scam, call the attorney general's office.
Xenophobia Scheme: "I'm from the police department and we caught a burglar in your neighborhood last night. I'd like to mark your valuables for you to avoid future losses."	The "law enforcement officer" is really a con artist who will lure you into revealing your valuables, then claim he left his engraver at the station. He takes them in order to mark them, never to return.	Always verify the law enforcement officer's identify by independently calling the station and never turn over valuables to anyone without a court order.	Contact your local police department if someone has approached you with this kind of pitch.
You Dented My Car Act: "Hey, is this your car? I got two witnesses that say you dented my side when you pulled into this parking spot. What are you gonna do about it?"	The con artist is staging this scene in order to intimidate you into paying a cash settlement for his dented car (which was already dented).	Don't be intimidated by such confrontational tactics. If this happens to you, offer to call the police. If it is a con, the schemer will flee in a hurry.	If you live in a city with bus service, you might consider taking the bus to the store. Also, consider taking a friend. This type of scam is much harder to pull on two people than on one person.
Zirconium Necklace Impostor: "You have just won a stunning two-carat diamond necklace. It is valued at over $750. All we need from you is a nominal mounting fee."	The "nominal fee" is often as much as $75 and the diamond necklace is a fake, worth less than $10.	Resist the "something for nothing" pitch. It is almost never worth the risk.	Report any such solicitation to the attorney general's office and if you have been taken, file a complaint with the attorney general.

THE TOP 10

FRAUD PREVENTION TIPS FOR OLDER ADULTS

1. Never participate in sweepstakes offers either through the mail or over the phone. The odds of winning are terrible and many are out and out scams.

2. Never buy anything over the phone unless you initiate the call. If a stranger calls you and asks you to buy or invest or donate, hang up the phone.

3. Shop in your own backyard. Decide what products you want and then find local merchants in the yellow pages to buy from.

4. Never make a buying decision based upon emotion. Don't let a salesperson convince you to "do it for your kids, or your grandkids."

5. Before buying from a business, find out:
- **The age** of the business
- **Where** it is located and for **how long**
- **Who** has done business there before and talk to them about the business
- **If any complaints** have been filed with the Better Business Bureau or the attorney general's office

6. Never buy anything from a door-to-door salesperson, especially someone purporting to be a contractor or a yard worker.

7. Never make a buying decision at the time of the sales pitch. Have your own personal rule that you have a three-day cooling off period before deciding whether or not to buy.

8. Before making a charitable contribution, ask for and review written financial reports of the charity to find out where your money is going.

9. Ask for advice from a friend or family member before deciding to buy something.

10. The most successful fraud pitch in the United States today is: CONGRATULATIONS, YOU'VE WON! Don't fall for it. There is nothing free in the marketplace and if someone tells you otherwise, the person is lying.

CHAPTER

4

FRAUD VICTIM CASE STUDIES

"You can fool too many of the people too much of the time."

—James Thurber

The best way to avoid becoming a fraud victim is to read about others' experiences with con artists. By seeing how the victim was approached and learning why he or she fell for it, you can avoid becoming a victim yourself. This chapter will outline five case studies of victims who fell for different pitches and lost various amounts of money. The important thing to think about when you read these accounts is, would I have spotted the scam before biting on it?

Here are some highlights from a poll commissioned by the National Consumer League in 1991. Did you know . . .

① 92 percent of Americans have, at one time or another, received a postcard or letter in the mail offering them a free prize? 29 percent of all American adults who have responded to these, or 53.6 million people, were scammed out of their money?

② 66 percent of the American public believes the elderly are most likely to be targeted as potential victims?

③ 31 percent (less than 1 in 3) reported the matter to authorities?

④ 34 percent (1 in 3) of American adults have been contacted by telephone about purchasing a financial investment? Over 90 percent of those contacted did not know the individual contacting them.

⑤ 17 percent (over 1 in 6) find it very difficult to resist a telephone solicitation?

⑥ Nearly 62 percent of the American public would not know where to call to find out if a telephone offer or promotion is legitimate?

⑦ In the past two years, 3 percent of American adults (or over 5.5 million people) have bought something by telephone that they now know was a definite fraud?

One way to ensure you will spot a scam before falling for it is to learn to identify common themes that are present in most fraud pitches. Let's look at some of these common themes before getting into individual victim case studies.

THE CLOAK OF LEGITIMACY

On the continuum of intelligence among criminals, you have bank robbers on one end, who go into a bank with a gun, go up to the bank teller and say, "Give me all your money or I'll blow your head off" with two cameras taking a picture of them. These are the dumbest criminals there are. Law enforcement catches 85 percent of bank robbers. On the opposite end of the continuum is the con artist, who also seeks to steal money, but does it by pretending to be an official from the bank trying to catch a dishonest bank employee or by offering free prizes or trips in exchange for buying overpriced vitamins.

Con artists understand that the best way to steal money and avoid prosecution is to pretend to be a legitimate business. By wrapping the "cloak of legitimacy" around themselves, con artists can convince victims to voluntarily turn over their money in the name of a legitimate business transaction.

This creates all kinds of challenges for law enforcement which must prove that the con artist had the "intent to defraud" his or her victim. Whereas the bank robber admits his evil intent on videotape, the con artist pretends to simply be a misunderstood businessperson. In order to prove the guilty intent, prosecutors must figure out a way to unwrap the cloak of legitimacy to reveal the operation's true intentions.

Every pitch, without exception, attempts to convince the victim that they are talking about a legitimate business opportunity. The cloak that con artists employ is often no more than a thin veil and can be removed by simply asking a few probing questions. Because the veil is so thin and so easily removed, any businessperson who is unwilling to answer your questions should be suspect. Legitimate businesses are proud of their company and are always willing to answer any and all questions.

THE SWEEPSTAKES MENTALITY

If I had to point to a single element found in most fraud schemes, it is the extent to which con artists seek to exploit the "sweepstakes mentality." The sweepstakes mentality is the pervasive belief (or hope) in American culture that it is possible to get something for nothing.

While most consumers are familiar with the phrase, "There is no such thing as a free lunch," there are many who simply forget the concept altogether when the fraudulent telemarketer calls.

Part of the reason why pitches seek to exploit the sweepstakes mentality is because both legitimate and illegitimate businesses use the free prize giveaway approach. From camping clubs and magazine sales to radio station promotions, American consumers cannot turn around without hearing about opportunities to "win" one fabulous prize or another. Even state governments promote (and exploit) the sweepstakes mentality by mounting massive advertising campaigns for lotteries. At last count, thirty-three out of fifty states had active state-sponsored lotteries.

When I asked John T. about the sweepstakes mentality, he said it was not just an important element, but was in fact the foundation of all of his pitches. "Whether you like it or not, people are always suckers for the something for nothing pitch. Call it greed or naiveté or just plain stupidity, all I know is it worked like a charm for me for ten years."

The fact that celebrities are on the air every other week handing some consumer a $10 million check, helps make believers out of thousands of prospective victims. I discuss throughout the book the concept of the consumer as mooch. The names of these people are coveted by con artists because they believe "once a mooch, always a mooch." Stated another way, "If he fell for it once, he'll fall for it again."

A major goal of this book is to convince consumers that any time they hear a sales pitch that includes words like "you have won" or "free prize" or "you're lucky," a red flag should go up.

THE CHARM FACTOR

In all the years I was a fraud investigator, every fraud victim I interviewed at some point told me, "I can't believe it, he seemed like such a nice man." Part of the 'trade' of being a con artist is to have an outgoing, friendly personality. In short, con artists are charming. After all, people don't give money to those they hate. Because many seniors live alone, they are extremely vulnerable to the smooth-talking, friendly ways of the con artist. Case studies described in this chapter document the loneliness factor as it pertains to victimization.

MR. PERSONALITY

In 1990 we were promoting the Stop Fraud Network throughout Washington State and a local Seattle television show called "Town Meeting" did an hour-long segment on fraud. John, Attorney General Ken Eikenberry, and I were all on, but John was clearly the star attraction.

After the show, the producer came up to him and said, "You know John, before the show started, the audience seemed hostile toward you.

But by the end of the show, I got the impression that they kind of liked you." John responded by saying, "If you had given me another hour, I would have been selling them investments."

The ability to quickly befriend people is characteristic of most con artists, both male and female. It is a characteristic that John has used throughout his career with great success and an element you will see in many of the pitches described.

NEWS EVENTS AS A "HOOK"

Another thread that runs through most fraud schemes is the tie to news events. In February 1991 John called me to say that his buddies who were still active in telemarketing fraud were begging him to get back into the business when the Persian Gulf War started.

When I asked him what the outbreak of war in the Persian Gulf had to do with getting back into the business, he said, "You've been a fraud investigator for how long Doug? You don't know nothing, do ya boy?"

John was giving me a hard time. He went on to explain that telemarketers are always looking for a new "hook" to get people's attention. Big news events like the war provide them with the perfect hook. "News legitimizes the pitch," John maintains. "Using the war as a hook, I could have sold gold coins, charitable solicitations, you name it. The trick is to just relate to what people are seeing on television and then build a pitch around it. The bigger the news story, the stronger the pitch."

THE FOLLOWER MENTALITY

John will tell you that another factor in pitching seniors is to exploit the "follower" mentality. This is the tendency, especially on the part of some older persons whose self-confidence has diminished, to do whatever a strong personality tells you to do. John told me the story of using the strong personality angle on a guy to sell him investments:

"I remember this as though it was yesterday. I was pitching this rich old guy in Kansas City. This would have been in about 1983 or 1984. I wanted to sell him badly because we were having an in-house competition that night to see who could bring in $25,000 first. So I'm telling him, 'Now Jim, we are offsetting on a four-corner situation and I have two shares reserved for you. The profit on this if it hits will be in the hundreds of thousands of dollars. The bottom line is I need $25,000 and I need it now!'

"I shut up and waited. You know the old saying about how you give your pitch, shut up and the first one who talks loses? Anyway he says something like, 'I'm sorry John but I just can't do that.' For some reason, I just decided to kick into high gear and, well, own the guy. I took the phone, held it about two feet away from me so that everyone in the boiler room would notice and watch the show and at the top of my lungs I started screaming into the phone, 'Don't you ever say no to me again! I will buy your shares, I will never call you back as long as I live, but don't you ever say no to me—and insult me like that, do you understand?'

"After my little tirade, the man apologized and said that he couldn't give me the $25,000 because there was a blinding snow storm in Kansas City that day, but he would go to his bank the next day and wire me the $25,000—which he did."

The con artist often will be very decisive and specific with his or her victim, much like John was in the above example. It is important to remember that some telemarketers and all con artists want only one thing: your money. Therefore, it is important to stand your ground and not give in.

"Con artists view consumers as sheep," John T. has said. "They are sheep waiting to be slaughtered."

If that statement doesn't convince you to hang up on suspicious-sounding telemarketers, nothing will. The next time strong-willed telemarketers call you, decide that they are the sheep and get them to "follow" your lead by hanging up the phone.

As you read through the victim case studies in this chapter, think about the five elements that seem to recur in fraud schemes:

① Cloak of legitimacy: pretending to be a legitimate business
② Sweepstakes mentality: believing you get something for nothing
③ Charm factor: falling prey to a con's charming personality
④ News as a hook: pitches tied to news events
⑤ Follower mentality: tendency to follow strong personalities

The number of cases which I have seen in thirteen years in the attorney general's office could fill literally thousands of pages. The examples that follow are therefore merely samples from among the endless cases of victimization which are reported each year.

MRS. CONNER

Companies that market living trusts to older Americans have proliferated throughout the nation in the past several years. These companies send salespeople, usually insurance agents, to seniors' homes to explain the "horrors" of probating a will and to pitch the living trust as the best way to avoid probate. A living trust is a legal document that if properly drafted and funded, will settle an estate outside of probate court. The trusts are appropriate for certain consumers but not all. It in effect allows a person to transfer all of his or her property and assets out of his or her will and into a trust which has a named beneficiary.

The effect of this transfer is that the consumer need not go through probate. The question of whether or not to execute a living trust, which can cost up to several thousand dollars, is determined by the size of your estate and where you live. Many states have streamlined probate laws which make probate quite inexpensive. In these states, a living trust may not save you money. In other states however, it may be helpful.

The problem is that there are literally thousands of salespersons marketing living trusts nationwide and claiming it will save them money, even though it won't.

Mrs. Conner is a typical victim of the living trust pitch. Mrs. Conner was a recent widow, eighty-two years old, and living by herself in a comfortable suburban community when a living trust company first called her. She received a call from a woman who said her organization was sending its advisors to explain new changes in the probate laws. Mrs. Conner asked if they were selling anything and the woman answered no, they just wanted to give her important information about the new laws.

The salesman who came to talk with Mrs. Conner was not there only to provide information. The salesman, Joe Turner, spent over four hours at Mrs. Conner's home trying to convince her that if she didn't have a living trust, her children would lose out on their inheritance because it would be consumed by fees of "greedy" lawyers, the probate court, and the federal government. Mr. Turner said lawyers would drag probate out as long as possible to justify high fees and the probate court would order her house locked up so even her children couldn't get in for years after she died. He also said estate taxes would take a big chunk of her assets.

Mr. Turner showed Mrs. Conner probate cases from California in which the fees totaled almost 50 percent of the estate. He also told her that if Howard Hughes and Marilyn Monroe would have had living trusts, their estates would have been settled in a fraction of the time instead of dragging on for years.

Although Mrs. Conner was frightened by Mr. Turner's statements, she found him to be very personable and reassuring. He had told Mrs. Conner it was apparent from how she talked about her family and all the photos in her home that she was a very devoted grandmother. He told her of his own wife and two young daughters and how he was struggling financially to be able to send them to ballet school and enable his wife to be home for the girls after school. Mrs. Conner said she felt Mr. Turner was completely trustworthy and genuinely concerned about her family.

Mrs. Conner said what eventually persuaded her to give Mr. Turner a $1,200 check for the living trust was his statement that she owed it to her children to make her estate settlement as easy and inexpensive as possible. She became worried that if she didn't have the living trust, her children and grandchildren would be left with nothing to inherit. Along with the $1,200 check, Mr. Turner took documents for Mrs. Conner's assets such as the deed to her home and investment statements which he explained they needed to prepare the trust.

Mrs. Conner had asked Mr. Turner for a few days to think it over and to talk to her oldest daughter about the living trust. But he insisted she had to buy the trust that day because he didn't know when he would be able to come back.

Mr. Turner returned to Mrs. Conner's home within a week. In this second visit, he explained that he had reviewed Mrs. Conner's investments and was concerned that she had not made wise choices in investing in stocks, bonds, and certificates of deposit. He advised her to transfer all of those investments, a total of $95,000, into tax-deferred annuities which he claimed were earning 8.5 percent interest. Mrs. Conner agreed to this transfer because Mr. Turner had stressed that she owed it to her children to make wise investments.

When Mrs. Conner later told her daughter, Sandra, about the living trust and annuity investments, Sandra suggested they talk to an attorney. The attorney reviewed the documents and said that the $1,200 Mrs. Conner spent on the living trust was about twice the amount it would have cost her to probate her estate with a will. The attorney explained that the salesman had greatly exaggerated the costs and time for probate, and apparently had failed to tell Mrs. Conner that federal estate tax is only assessed if your estate exceeds $600,000.

The attorney explained that the annuities were not as great as the salesman had led Mrs. Conner to believe as they had costly early withdrawal penalties and the interest rate could be lowered after the first year. She also cautioned Mrs. Conner that it was risky to invest so much of her money in one type of investment.

Sandra was concerned that investing the $95,000 in the annuities had virtually locked up her mother's money for ten years. Mrs. Conner had only $2,500 in a checking account which could have been quickly exhausted with an unexpected car or house repair.

Mrs. Conner was able to get the money in the annuities returned due to a refund provision in the state insurance law. However, the company refused to refund the $1,200 for the living trust.

Mrs. Conner's experience highlights several methods slick salespeople use with older Americans: gaining their trust, playing on emotions about their family, and pressuring them into making quick decisions.

Mrs. Conner should have followed her first instinct which was to take her time to think it over and talk to her children. In doing so, she would have avoided all the stress this incident caused her. As with any purchase involving estate settlement or preparation of a legal document, Mrs. Conner should have consulted with an attorney before writing the check.

If you receive a call from someone claiming to be from a retirement organization, be aware that it could be a salesperson selling living trusts. The best protection against situations like the one that happened to Mrs. Conner is to never allow salespersons to come into your home. If you are concerned that a living trust might benefit you and your heirs, call your attorney, make an appointment to go to his or her office and spend thirty minutes or so discussing it. Even if it costs you $50 to $75, it's money well spent to get objective, sound advise.

MRS. ANDERSON

Mrs. Anderson, like Mrs. Conner, fits the profile of the potentially most vulnerable victim. She was seventy-nine years old, widowed, and living alone when her daughter called my office in April 1990. Her daughter, Jill Becker, had called us because she had seen John T. on a local television program the previous evening discussing how telefrauders target older adults.

Jill told me her mother seemed to be living on her own quite well. Her father had died about five years before and, unlike some women of her era, her mother had a working knowledge of the household's finances at the time of her husband's death.

Jill did say that her mother had called from time to time and expressed a sense of being bored, which Jill had interpreted as being lonely. Jill recalls discussing with her mom possible activities she could become involved in to keep busy. But each time she mentioned one of them her mother had an answer for why she couldn't possibly do it.

"What about volunteering at the local senior center?" Jill recalls asking her mother.

"Oh, I don't know anyone down there. Besides, I've driven by there before and there are nothing but old people who go there," said her mother.

"How about going to your local elementary school and volunteering? You used to teach school, Mom. It would be the perfect way to keep busy. And they need your help," said Jill.

"And be around all those screaming kids all day long? No thanks. I had enough of that during my twenty years as a school teacher in the classroom," her mother retorted.

Jill gave up on finding an activity for her mother after encountering such consistent resistance.

When Jill called, she told me that her mother had been contacted three years ago by a man named Jim Kaiser. Mr. Kaiser was calling her to talk about investing in commodities and precious metals. Jill told me that Kaiser began to call her mother every day, not necessarily to sell her investments, but simply to chat. He was a friendly, charming voice on the phone to a woman who very few people called, especially since her husband died.

Jill said that over time, Mr. Kaiser began to tell Mrs. Anderson about a rich millionaire friend of his who had died and left him as the sole owner of a nationwide baby food company. He told her the estate was being tied up in probate and he was having trouble paying his portion of the attorney's fees and the cost of hiring guards to protect the plant.

Jill indicated that her mother had received a $100,000 life insurance payoff when her husband died. Kaiser, over this three-year period he had been talking with Mrs. Anderson, convinced her that if she would help pay for part of the probate costs, he would make her vice-president of the company. Jill said her mother had given Kaiser the entire $100,000 death benefit received when her husband died.

In the meantime, Jill had discovered through the authorities that this Mr. Kaiser was a convicted drug dealer. When she confronted her mother with that fact, her mother knew all about it and defended Kaiser.

"Oh Jill, Jim told me all about that. You see, several years ago, he got into a terrible automobile accident. While he was in the hospital, he became addicted to morphine and had a few problems, but it wasn't his fault." Mrs. Anderson refused to listen to her daughter's concerns and lost $100,000 in the process.

Whether one wishes to call this the "love con" or perhaps simply the "infatuation con," this example demonstrates a number of things. First, Mrs. Anderson refused to stop talking to Kaiser. It was almost as though she paid $100,000 for a friend to call her on the phone over this period of time. As it turns out, there was no baby food company, there was no dead millionaire, there were no expensive lawyer's fees. Furthermore, her daughter Jill, upon further investigation, discovered that Kaiser was wanted by the FBI for mail and wire fraud.

Mrs. Anderson was less a victim of the sweepstakes mentality here, although she was promised a prominent position in the nonexistent corporation. Instead, she was a victim of loneliness and the con man's ability to charm his victim and convince her to do things which would have otherwise been against her better judgment. Needless to say, she never got her $100,000 back.

In retrospect, Jill Becker wishes she had been more persistent in the months following her father's death in forcing her mother to get involved in some activity.

"Instinctively, I knew Mom had to find an activity, which is why I suggested the senior center or volunteering at the school. But when she showed no interest, I just gave up. I should have tried harder, I guess."

Jill did the best she could do under the circumstances and, quite frankly, more than many sons or daughters do for newly widowed parents. It was really her mother who might have done things differently. Jill told me while her mother refused to file a complaint against Kaiser, she was quite upset when Kaiser stopped calling her, and this occurred right around the time she had run out of money.

Ultimately, everyone must decide how to run his or her own life, whether the person is young or old, married or single, or some combination of the two. If, upon reading this account, your blood boils half as much as mine did, you will take it upon yourself to make sure the Jim Kaisers of the world don't swindle someone you know.

MRS. CHAMBERS

The sale of Medicare supplement (or Medigap) insurance policies to older persons presents a keen example of con artists' ability to manipulate their victims.

Medigap insurance is designed to provide coverage to persons over sixty-five years of age who are eligible for Medicare. Medicare pays 80 percent of the allowable medical bills for eligible seniors. This means that most seniors need an additional insurance policy to cover the 20 percent "gap" not covered by Medicare.

Throughout the 1980s, there were numerous unscrupulous practices employed by insurance salespeople to sell these policies to seniors. One of the cases I worked on occurred around the time the new Catastrophic Care Act (which was later repealed) had passed through Congress.

There was an insurance agency at the time that had set up a huge telephone boiler room to generate leads for their 180 salespeople statewide who were on the street selling Medigap insurance policies. They would call a senior from a list they had purchased from a market research company. The caller would give the following pitch:

"Hello, Mrs. Chambers, this is Joan Biglow. I am calling from the American Retired Person's Association. I'm calling to let you know that there are a lot of important issues we're working on here at our association. And we'd like to come out to your house and explain some of the things going on with Medicare and the new Catastrophic Care Act. Now we're going to have someone in your neighborhood tomorrow around 11:00 A.M. Will you be available at that time?"

This pitch was used to get the salesperson a foot in the door. The insurance companies were taking an issue which at the time was being discussed and written about every day in the news media and telling the victim it was going to affect him or her, and that the insurance company had the solution.

The use of the retirement association is another ploy to get in the door because most seniors who agree to such appointments do not think an insurance salesperson is coming to their door. Rather, they think it is an independent retirement association.

In this particular case, I was able to conduct an undercover investigation. A woman named Mrs. Chambers had received a phone call similar to the above pitch. Mrs. Chambers, like Mrs. Conner and Mrs. Anderson, was also a widow. She lived by herself in a charming house in an upscale section of Magnolia, a suburb of Seattle.

Unlike the two previous fraud victims, Mrs. Chambers was a very savvy consumer who was not about to be taken by anyone. She had been skeptical when the call came offering a visit from the retirement association. So skeptical in fact that she asked the caller three different times if he was going to try to sell her anything. Three different times he said he would not be selling anything, he just wanted to talk about the benefits of the association and the Catastrophic Care Act.

Mrs. Chambers finally agreed to let him come to her home the next day at 11:00 A.M. after being told he would not be selling anything. When she hung up the phone, she looked up the name "Association of Retired Americans" in the phone book. When she couldn't find the name, she became very suspicious and called the attorney general's office.

I interviewed her and after hearing what had happened asked her if I could come out to her house the next day posing as her son to see just exactly what the salesman was up to. She agreed to do this.

The next day came and the person she was going to meet with got there early. She had expected a nice gray-haired gentleman to come call on her and talk about Congress and how the new Catastrophic Care Act would affect her. Instead the man who showed up was a tall, dark-skinned thirty-year-old. She let him in knowing that I would be arriving any minute.

Even though Mrs. Chambers had never met me before, she played it like a pro. When I arrived about five minutes later, she greeted me with a very sincere, "Oh son, come in . . . he's already here!"

With that, I introduced myself and sat down at the dining room table to listen to this guy's story. It turns out that he had one goal in mind: he was there to sell Medigap and nursing home insurance. For the better part of an hour, he hammered Mrs. Chambers. "What would happen to you if you had a stroke tomorrow? Could you afford $30,000 a year in nursing home bills? Could you?" he said looking at me.

I sat through the entire presentation without letting on who I was. After I got back to the office, I checked out the name of the insurance agency which the salesman worked for. It turns out that this agency had just recently been reprimanded by the state insurance commissioner's office thirty days before for the same practice: lying to seniors over the phone in order to get an in-home appointment.

This case illustrates one way unscrupulous salespeople have of manipulating consumers. Not only did the salesman gain entry under false pretenses, but he was a very imposing figure. At times, he would raise his voice and lean over the table toward Mrs. Chambers as a method of intimidation. And that was with me there! What would he have done if I hadn't been there? Many seniors will do whatever a salesman like that tells them to do in that situation.

Older adults purchase over $4 billion worth of unnecessary medical insurance each year. One reason for that is the ease with which unscrupulous salespeople can enter the home under false pretenses and then convince them to buy. Because so many seniors live by themselves, it is easy for con artists to isolate their victims and take their money the way the salesman attempted to do to Mrs. Chambers.

Mrs. Chambers however did exactly what she was supposed to do. She made the mistake of agreeing to the appointment, but upon realizing her mistake, she called the authorities. As a result, she not only prevented herself from being isolated and possibly ripped off, but she also enabled the state to sue the firm in question for violation of the state consumer protection act.

In addition, several months after our lawsuit was filed, we made a video about fraud and Mrs. Chambers became the heroine of the video. She agreed to help us film a reenactment of the undercover investigation so others could see how to handle such a situation.

You might say Mrs. Chambers is one of the original American fraud fighters. More on this in chapter 7.

JOHN AND MARTHA SIMONSON

John and Martha Simonson had been retired for about three years when they had their first encounter with unscrupulous sales techniques.

In the mid-1980s, there was a firm called Cashsavers, Inc. This company sent out ten thousand flyers per week informing consumers that they were "absolutely guaranteed to win either $10,000 in cash or a new BMW." The flyers also listed several other prizes which the consumers could win if they were willing to come listen to a short sales presentation.

This company was getting as many as two hundred people per week coming into their offices to claim their prizes. The firm claimed it could save consumers up to 80 percent off the purchase of major products of all kinds because they go directly to the manufacturers, thereby cutting out the middle men which would save consumers money.

The pitch included the drop close described in chapter 2. The person explains that the normal price for this membership is $4,000, but since the company is having a special promotion, there is a 50 percent discount if the consumer purchases a membership on his or her first visit to the office. As with camping club promotions, the salespersons are instructed to "build value" by presenting an artificially inflated regular price, then drop it to encourage consumers to buy immediately or on their first visit.

The Simonsons visited Cashsavers headquarters one day in response to the flyer they had received offering the new BMW and $10,000. "We didn't really expect to receive these expensive prizes. But we were curious what this was all about and since we had time on our hands, we went in."

When they heard about all the money they could save, they decided to spend the $2,000 it cost to join. "We were in the market to buy a new refrigerator, and they asked us how much we expected to pay. When I told them the ones we were looking at cost around $900, they said the buying club could get it for $399. That was very attractive," Mrs. Simonson said.

John and Martha were not the only consumers who fell for this sales pitch. The company took in over $800,000 in nine months from consumers before we shut the operation down and they filed bankruptcy. Unfortunately, most of the money they took in was spent by the owner and his friends. Needless to say, John and Martha didn't get a dime back.

The attorney general's office sued the company for a number of reasons. First, no consumer ever received either $10,000 in cash or a new BMW. What the consumer received was a travel coupon for five days, four nights in Hawaii (accommodations only). The ex-office manager of this firm told me that the owner paid $5.00 for each travel coupon, even though he told consumers on his mailer the vacation was worth $395. He paid only $5.00 because very few consumers actually went to Hawaii to use the coupons since they would have to fly there at their own expense to do so.

The second problem was that they were not able to save consumers anywhere near 80 percent on purchases. Consumers who did join and try to use the buying club directory of manufacturing contacts were told they had never heard of the firm. The company had simply looked up the home office of major manufacturers and put them together in a book.

When this firm closed up shop and moved to Oregon to begin operations, the officials in that state sued and at the trial, the ex-office manager said that the owner had been promising color televisions as a free prize. What he didn't tell them was that only one in ten thousand people actually won.

In the Oregon trial, the ex-office manager testified that one day a consumer came in and actually had the winning number. So he went to the owner and said, "Jim, there's a guy out there who has the winning number. That means we're going to have to give him a television. But that should be no problem because we can buy one through our buying club, right?" To which the owner responded, "No way, that would be way too expensive, let's go to the nearest discount store and buy one."

The moral of this story is that businesses that promise absurdly attractive offers are almost always lying—it's that simple.

In this example, huge throngs of consumers of all ages came to Cashsavers to do what? To pick up their $10,000 check or their new car. The question everyone should ask upon hearing such a sales pitch is, How can any business afford to hand out checks for $10,000 in cash?

The answer, upon reflection, is "They can't." Unfortunately people see advertisements for state-sponsored lotteries and other "legal" prize promotions every day of their lives. This tends to cloud their otherwise sound judgment about the possibilities of getting a huge windfall. The bottom line is if someone writes or calls you and says, "You've won!" tell the person to get lost!

MR. AND MRS. McNEAL

Mr. and Mrs. McNeal were retired teamsters who had a decent income. One day, Mr. McNeal was sitting at home watching television when he opened that day's mail and it said that he and his wife had been selected as a finalist in a grand prize giveaway. The mailer listed several prizes including a brand new Ford Bronco. Mr. McNeal was instructed by the mailer to call the phone number in Las Vegas to determine if he had won the grand prize.

When he showed the mailer to his wife, they got excited and thought to themselves, maybe we really have won. They thought it sounded a lot like those other sweepstakes they had seen on television with a celebrity handing the lucky winners a check for $10 million. So they picked up the phone and made the long distance call to Las Vegas. A woman answered the phone and asked Mrs. McNeal for the registration number in the upper left hand corner of the mailer. Mrs. McNeal read her number and she then put Mrs. McNeal on hold. She came back after a few minutes and let out a scream and said, "Congratulations. You are our grand prize winners. You've won the Bronco!!!"

The McNeals naturally became very excited and the woman on the other end kept that enthusiasm going right into the part about the special deal they had going on water purification systems. The pitch was very smooth according to the victims.

"She was a very nice person and we were excited because we had just won a new car. She started talking to us about the Pacific Northwest where we live. She said she thought it was a beautiful area up there and how she had a sister who lived there. She said her sister had complained that the water pollution problem was getting bad and she had to go buy a water filtration system because she was afraid her kids would get sick if they continued to drink the water.

"The lady continued on to say that she was angry with her sister because her company carries water filtration devices and she could have gotten one from her at half the normal price. One thing led to another and before you know it, she was talking us into buying a water filter for $359. We thought to ourselves, What's $359 when we have just won a $15,000 new car? So we paid for the water filter and you know something? We have never gotten our Ford Bronco or any gift for that matter."

The McNeals readily admit they got sucked in by the idea of getting something for nothing. They had never previously considered buying a water filtration device nor had they even asked to participate in a sweepstakes. But when they were told they had been the lucky winners, they lost their objective reasoning ability and were therefore vulnerable to a clever and rather aggressive sales pitch.

This example is typical of the way con artists manipulate the sweepstakes mentality in order to sell overpriced or nonexistent products. Consumers are bombarded with news and government-sponsored messages about winning to the extent that when a phony contest is presented showing them as the winners, they tend to believe it. As I said before, if someone tells you you've won, tell the person to get lost.

All of the victims profiled in this chapter were relatively intelligent, decent folks who simply got caught off guard and became fraud victims.

It is difficult to estimate how many Mrs. Conners or Mrs. Andersons are out there being taken each year, because often such crimes are not reported to authorities. Even when they are reported, law enforcement is rarely successful at recouping what has been lost. The key is prevention: don't fall for companies like Cashsavers or people like Jim Kaiser no matter how alluring the pitch might be.

TOP FRAUDS TODAY

Remember that frauders practice all the ABC's of fraud you learned in the last chapter. Learn the fraud pitches in this book and you will be able to spot these scammers, even as they develop new-and-improved con schemes. The stories change; the basics remain the same.

The current trend of telephone fraud is also among the most wicked and devious. Law enforcement has nicknamed these pitches "rip and tear," as the victims never receive anything.

Frauders are calling people who have been victimized before over the telephone, usually by the "one of four" prize scam. These callers are identifying themselves as either collection/recovery services or as attorneys. These pitches stretch the imagination, yet they work. The scamsters get additional money from people who have already been victimized. The average victim seems to be the older adult, a person in his or her sixties, seventies, or eighties.

➻ THE RIP AND TEAR "RECOVER YOUR LOSSES" SCHEME

THE PITCH

"I am calling from American Recovery Services, Inc. Our investigations show that you have been the victim of fraudulent telephone sales. You were promised that you would receive thousands of dollars worth of prizes, but you never got them. Am I right?

"By law these companies do not have to post surety bonds to do business. We have frozen the accounts of over twenty different telephone operations and are in the process of making sure that the people who lost their money to these companies get their money back. You would like to get all the money back that you sent to these people, right?

"How many companies have you sent money to? What are the names of these companies and the approximate dollar amount you lost? We guarantee that you will receive your money back. Now, by law we do charge you a processing fee of $1,000. We need $500 up front, and you can pay the other $500 once you receive your refund checks. Fair enough?"

THE RESULT

You will receive nothing. While there are some states that require telemarketing organizations to be registered with them, these states have neither the budget, nor the employees, to investigate the companies that register with them.

PREVENTION TIP

When you realize this pitch is being given, get the frauder's name, business name, address, and telephone number. Tell the frauder that this sounds good but you need everything in writing first. At this time you will be pressured—the frauder will tell you there is some reason why you must act now.

However, demand to see the offer in writing before you send a penny. If you feel you are being pressured too much, tell the phone frauder that someone is at the door, or that you have to let the dog out, or some other excuse to leave the telephone. Set your receiver on the table for fifteen minutes and then hang up the telephone. Do not answer your telephone for at least an hour after you hang it up.

WHERE TO GO FOR HELP

If you did not fall for this pitch, call the National Consumer's Fraud Complaint Center and tell them of this call. If you receive verification of what the caller said in writing through the U.S. mail, whether or not you fell victim to this, notify your regional U.S. postal inspector. Remember, even though the scammer sends you the pitch in writing, it is still a scam. If you have sent money, make a complaint to the attorney general's office and your regional FBI office.

➡ *THE RIP AND TEAR "ATTORNEY PRIZE AWARD" SCAM*

THE PITCH

"This is John Jones, attorney at law. We represent XYZ bonding company, the company that insured the million-dollar prize giveaway for ABC Company. ABC has gone out of business and as a result the prize distribution is being handled by our law firm.

"It appears that you were awarded the second prize of $20,000. We believe the company was attempting to keep the money themselves, but since our firm took over their finances, we are required to finish the prize giveaway on behalf of XYZ bonding company, which wrote the surety bond and guaranteed this promotion and your prize. I need your full legal name, social security number, and current mailing address so I can release this check to you.

"You will be receiving a 1099 form, as a gift tax is due and payable on this prize during your next tax cycle. You know, you can't escape taxes. Now, I will also need for you to pay our attorney's supervision fee of $1,500 before my firm will allow me to release the check to you. . . ."

THE RESULT

People who believe this pitch also receive nothing. As a matter of fact, these criminals are becoming more and more brazen. I know of an instance that occurred in November 1993 in which the phone frauder actually spoke with the victim's bank manager and convinced the bank that he was an attorney and that the promotion was legitimate. The bank manager then approved the $1,500 bank wire to go into the con artist's bank account.

PREVENTION TIP

It is a federal sweepstakes law that if you win a prize you do not have to pay anything to get it. When you realize this pitch is being given, get the frauder's name, business name, address, telephone number, and state bar license number. Tell the frauder that this sounds good but you need everything in writing first. Tell the frauder you will be calling his or her state's attorney licensing section (normally the state bar). Do not, under any circumstances, send the frauder money. You can pretend you are going to follow through with the frauder's instructions and call your regional FBI office. Remember, these frauders can be quite convincing. If you feel yourself succumbing to the pressure to send money, hang up the telephone.

WHERE TO GO FOR HELP

If you did not fall for this pitch call the National Consumer's Fraud Complaint Center and tell them of this call. If you received any notification through the U.S. mail, notify your regional U.S. postal inspector. Otherwise, contact the FBI, the attorney general's office in your state, and the attorney general's office in the state you were contacted from.

Make your complaints as soon as possible. Con artists who use this scam normally move around a lot and typically are working alone, or with small groups of mobile swindlers.

Business Opportunities

There are many gray areas in the arena of business opportunities. These frauders target laid-off defense workers, other unemployed professionals, and seniors. The con is simple. You invest your money to start your own business, one you can operate from home. You will make a great living if you stick with it. These pitches range from sounding like believable business opportunities to pie in the sky chances.

☆ Pay telephones
☆ Amusement video games
☆ Charity honor boxes
☆ Mortgage finders
☆ Home computer employment
☆ Own your own 900 number
☆ Lost money searches
☆ Direct mail catalog companies

Free Prize, or Guaranteed Award

These have moved more toward mass mailer call-ins, although there are many boiler rooms that still call. The mass mailer announces you are guaranteed an award, all you have to do is call the 800 or 900 number. When you call the frauder asks you for the award number that is imprinted on the certificate. When you say the number, you are told you are a winner and you will be receiving a guaranteed award. The caller goes on to explain that the next drawing has even better prizes and to enter that one all you have to do is buy a water filter, vitamins, or other merchandise.

Investments

This is an area where many of the scams used in the past are starting to resurface. One illusion, the sunken treasure routine, is back again. This one has been used for hundreds (maybe thousands) of years, yet it comes back like a bad penny. Armed with maps and scuba gear the frauders find investors through advertisements placed in the newspapers and through referrals of people who have already invested. Sunken treasures found in the last ten years are the hook. Once again, modern technology is enabling you to make your dreams come true.

The 1960s was a great time for land scams. Normally this was in the California desert or the swamps of Florida. They are back again. One example is the helicopter ride hook, in Florida. Scammers find swamp land outside of Orlando and then take the marks on a helicopter ride to see the land, if the mark wants to fly to Orlando and see it. The frauders will put the mark, and the family, up at Disneyworld for a couple of days. This puts them in a good mood. Then they are taken on the helicopter, which speeds up to make it seem the land is closer to civilization than it is. The scammers show development maps and expound on the story that Disneyworld used to be a swamp.

Another popular scheme in the 1960s was the mining for gold in the sea. The popularity of Sea Lab helped tremendously. Water could be vacuumed from the sea and the gold extracted to make a huge profit. Modern technology was the pitch. Today the 'mining for precious metals in the sea' scam is starting to surface again.

It may seem odd but whenever the government has anything to do with offerings to the public a major heyday is had for the frauders. In the early 1980s it was an opportunity at winning an oil lease, today it is wireless cable. The scams normally go like this: You have a chance at obtaining a government license to own wireless cable in a certain area or you can invest with someone who has a license as part of an investment group. The top investment fraud picks of the 1990s include:

- ✍ Wireless cable
- ✍ Rare coins
- ✍ Desert or swamp land
- ✍ Sea water mining
- ✍ Precious metals

Mail Fraud

Work-at-home mailers and the free prize (or award) are still the hottest tickets going. Psychic and astrologer mailers are also very prevalent. Beware of anything that is made to look like a government envelope. Watch out for offers for credit cards or mortgage loans.

TOP PICKS FOR THE FUTURE

The 1990s are sure to see some of these scams making their way into living rooms across America:

✔ Domestic gas drilling, uncapping, or buying of wells: This will happen should the government decide to raise incentives for the use and/or exploration of natural gas.

✔ When Europe releases the Eurodollar there will be a flood of phone rooms switching over to this. It may even replace precious metals in rooms for awhile.

✔ Investments in Russian diamonds: Phone scammers will tell you Russians are leaving the country with diamonds. You can get a great deal, but you have to keep your mouth shut about it. Scammers will also tell you that you can make cash money off this.

✔ Private stock or percentage partnership in a manufacturing plant in Mexico, because the North American free trade agreement was reached.

✔ New inventions, high-tech breakthroughs: This one hasn't really been used successfully since the "talking typewriters" of the 1960s. It's coming back. Maybe this time it will be, "Own your own functioning robot."

THE TOP 10

PERSONAL SAFETY TIPS FOR OLDER ADULTS

1. Keep your doors and windows locked at all times. On a warm weather day, don't leave a side door open.

2. Have keys ready when approaching your home.

3. If you arrive home to find that windows or doors have been tampered with, don't go inside but, instead, call the police from a neighbor's house.

4. If someone arrives unexpectedly at your house, find out who it is before opening the door. Install a peephole in the door.

5. Record only nonspecific messages on your answering machine and avoid messages like, "We'll be back at 7:00 P.M. on Sunday."

6. Don't give personal information to unknown callers. If you receive a obscene or crank call, hang up immediately, saying nothing.

7. When walking, choose busy streets and avoid passing vacant lots, alleys, or deserted construction sites. At night, walk only in well-lighted areas and try to avoid walking or jogging alone.

8. Carry a purse close to your body and avoid wrapping the strap around your arm or hand. Carry a wallet in an inside coat pocket or front trouser pocket.

9. In an elevator, stand in easy reach of the floor selection panel.

10. On the street, when two or more people are coming toward you, always walk around them rather than between them.

THE TOP 10

HOME SECURITY TIPS FOR OLDER ADULTS

1. Install adequate exterior lighting at all entrances, near the garage, and in the garden. This is one of the most important burglary deterrents. To conserve energy, consider using photoelectric sensors.

2. For exterior doors, install solid-core wood doors with rugged frames that cannot be spread apart with a pry bar. A single cylinder dead bolt with a one-inch throw, in addition to the key-in-the-knob lock, is essential.

3. Keep windows closed and locked when you are away from the house. Windows should have auxiliary locking devices. Screens and storm windows should be securely fastened to the structure.

4. Consider installing an alarm system. Your local crime prevention officer can assist you with information.

5. Prune any shrubs or trees that obscure doors and windows.

6. Avoid hiding your extra set of house keys under the doormat or in a flower pot—that's the first place burglars look! Instead, give your keys to a trusted neighbor.

7. Always keep garage doors closed and locked. You don't want a burglar having access to your tools and ladders to aid him or her breaking into your home!

8. Leave some interior lights on when you are away from home.

9. Secure sliding glass doors with commercially available bars or locks, or put a wooden dowel or broomstick in the door track.

10. Engrave your valuable property, such as televisions, VCR's, computers, cameras and stereos, with your driver's license number.

AND . . . WHEN YOU GO AWAY

1. Have a neighbor collect your mail and newspapers daily.

2. Avoid leaving a message on your answering machine indicating that you are away.

3. Put an automatic timer on some interior lights. Use photoelectric sensors to turn exterior lights on and off automatically.

4. Leave a radio on.

5. Tell a trusted neighbor your departure and return dates. Include an itinerary and phone numbers where you can be reached in case of an emergency.

THE TOP 10

CHARITABLE SOLICITATION TIPS FOR OLDER ADULTS

1. To avoid problems with people asking for charitable donations, establish an annual charitable giving plan at the beginning of each year. Decide how much and to whom you will give and then investigate those charities before giving. Whenever others call throughout the year, tell them to send you written information so that you can consider them next year.

2. Before giving to a charity, ask for printed materials through the mail that include the name, address, and telephone number of the charity.

3. Before giving, ask for a statement that describes how and where the funds will be used and a copy of the fund-raiser/charity's registration number (where applicable).

4. Before giving, ask for a statement that describes how much of the money you give goes to charitable purpose versus to the fund-raiser.

5. Before giving, ask for a description of the charity's fund-raising history, including information about how they have spent their money in the past.

6. Before giving, make sure you have verified the information they have sent you by contacting either your secretary of state's office or your local attorney general's office. In most states, one of these agencies requires annual financial reports that disclose how charitable organizations spend their money.

7. Never respond to an emotional plea from a caller who is appealing for funds to help victims of a natural disaster or a war or some other major news event. Always demand that such callers send you written information before you consider giving.

8. Never send cash to a charity either through the mail or at your door. Always write a check and state on the check what it is for.

9. Don't respond to high pressure sales tactics. Always give yourself ample time to think about it before giving.

10. If you suspect fraud or have questions about a solicitation you receive over the phone or through the mail, contact your state attorney general or secretary of state's office.

THE TOP 10

INVESTMENT FRAUD TIPS FOR OLDER ADULTS

Before making an investment of any size, ask yourself the following questions:

1. How long has the firm been in business?

2. Is the firm based or do they have offices in your community?

3. Is the investment firm willing to supply you with a list of clients who have done business with them in the past?

4. Are you willing to call several people on that list to ask about the firm's performance?

5. Is the firm licensed with appropriate state agencies and will they provide you with evidence of such licensure(s)?

6. Have you called the securities department or the attorney general's office in your state to verify their licensure status?

7. If the firm has been in business less than one year, is it a good idea to do business with them? Should you consider going with a firm that has a more established track record?

8. Before investing, will you have your attorney or accountant review the terms of the investment?

9. Is the firm willing to put all representations they make regarding the investments in writing?

10. Is it your policy to never invest in anything over the phone, no matter how convincing the person on the other end sounds?

PROFILE OF A CON ARTIST

"Everybody's so determined to being greedy, to being ignorant. Maybe what they need is a little . . . liberalized education. So, in order to teach 'em I qualified myself with an honorary degree—Mortechi Jones, M.B.S.C.S.D.D. Master of Back Stabbin', Cork Screwin', and Dirty Deals. Ours is a society of goods and services and I think I'm performing a service. 'Cause after meeting up with me they ain't so eager for the edge the next time."

—George C. Scott, in *The Flimflam Man*

There is one primary characteristic of con men and women: they are lazy. They want to get money without working hard and so they look for the easiest victims to swindle. The con artist targets older persons because he or she perceives this group as more gullible and therefore more easily conned. The techniques or pitches used focus on telling the victim that he or she will get more money or save more money by hiring the person. In this chapter, we outline five con artists' operations and explain who they went after and how they did it. The schemes involve siding sales, cassette tapes, real estate investments, transient blacktop pavers, and master recording investments.

One trait common to con artists is their belief that they are actually "helping" their victims. John T. tells of how he actually talked himself into believing he was helping people by deceiving them. "I told my friends that I was actually helping enhance their lives. Without me they would not be able to live the glorious adventures of the financial world. I went with them to South Africa to explore the diamond mines, I took them to the oil wells to feel the exhilaration of hitting a gusher-liquid gold. These people witnessed instant wealth, looking out over the 640 acres of gas well country they had won in the government's lease lottery. I brought them back into history to savor the minting of a coin and its history. I taught them the intricacies of attending estate sales and how to pick out, negotiate, and sell the 'high quality' Morgan silver dollars and St. Gaudin gold coins. My patrons attended art gallery exhibit openings with me and they sat in at the 'back-room' meetings, where the real business of art is carefully manipulated. I took my clients on adventures, adventures in life they could find nowhere else. I was friend, psychologist, and business advisor all wrapped up in one. Of course they had to pay top dollar for this service. The service I provided was well worth it. The service I provided gave them life, gave them hope."

FRAUDER
1) A person who uses unlawful or immoral deception to steal from others.

A frauder is also known to law enforcement as a confidence artist, larcenist, smooth-talking bandit, flim-flam man, bamboozler, hornswoggler, con artist, thief, robber, antagonist, pilferer, cheater, stealer, purloiner, mesmerizer, antagonist, impostor, swindler.

They tend to be loners, however they are people who have the ability to make many friends and acquaintances. They are known to be charming and interesting. They display impulsive acts and can lie, steal, vandalize and be aggressive against others, to the point of harm. The rights of others are of no concern to them and they act emotionally indifferent. They show great mood swings at times and perceive reality differently than most people. Their reality is to the point of delusion, for they have justified their actions to the extreme. Above all, they know how to make us feel we are "special."

Frauders are normally men and women you enjoy spending a lot of time with. They have great stories and they listen to your stories, with appreciation. Little do you realize it but as you tell them a story of your life, they are analyzing your weak points, ready to move in for the kill. By the time you are done "spilling your guts" to the con artist you are like a wounded deer standing on your last legs in a forest. The hunter has you in his sights and he is ready to pull the trigger.

The behavioral personality of a frauder is not to feel emotions, except for exhilaration (at taking you for your money), ego, anger, and a sense of victory. Many feel a sense of relief when they make money, it keeps them supplied with the drugs of their choice. Whether you are mortgaging your home or tapping into your savings the swindler does not care. Victory is the crime.

Most frauders start in the fraud business not knowing they are lying. A majority of frauders get their initial start in boiler rooms (telephone sales). The boiler rooms separate the new salespeople from the experienced frauder. The potential frauders are placed in what is called a 'front room' and are instructed to dial and smile, read the presentation word for word and to call for the manager if they are having problems. About one out of twenty new salespeople make it to being a frauder.

The process of becoming a frauder is devious. The salesperson is conned by management into believing the presentation is real, that the corporation has made so much money that year they have to give away prizes for their taxes. The salesperson believes what he or she is saying. The ones who go on to become frauders are the best salespeople, the ones who have natural ability and are willing to learn. John T. entered into telemarketing like this and made $1,100 his second week, in 1978. His story is remarkably similar to that of his previous peer group.

John T. explains, "There I was, in Las Vegas. I sold a lot that day and my sales manager invited me out for a night on the town with the 'pros', the salesmen I idolized. Dave took me to a party with Lorenzo,

Wild Willy, and Tommy. They were in their late twenties to early forties and I felt as if I were part of a family. These men took me under their wings. They called me 'kid', I was the wonder boy. I got the attention I had desired all these years. Suddenly I was important, I was special. The girls at the company thought I was important. As time went by many high-power frauders became my mentors. During my fourth and fifth years in the 'telemarketing advertising specialty business' (phone fraud) there were at least three parties a week, gatherings of at least thirty or forty 'telephone salespeople' and secretaries. When I would walk in the door I was hailed, praised by my fellows, given drugs and women. Who among us does not desire to be important, to be noticed, to be favored, to be financially secure? These confidence artists gave me all this and more. They showed me the ways of the world, the asphalt jungle. They accepted me as one of them, a part of their family of frauders.

MOOCH
1) A person who wants "something for nothing."

2) A person who cannot say no to a sales or fraud pitch, when pressured.

3) Frauder slang. An idiot who says yes when you do the pitch right.

A mooch is also known to frauders as a sucker, pawn, pansy, wimp, fool, chump, dupe, easy mark, fall guy, fish, patsy, pigeon, sap, victim, stooge, trick, nincompoop, casualty, dummy, pawn, puppet.

The universal motivation used by these silver-tongued devils is greed. Greed stays a vicious emotion, never being satisfied. The frauder knows this and will start by dialing g for greed, either you have won a prize or you can make a lot of money or you can get the deal of a lifetime. If you are what the frauders term a mooch, you will fall for the scam with very little trouble. You actually believe what this person has said. True mooches account for only about 10 percent of sales.

Over the years the bamboozlers have discovered that most victims do have some type of defense system. This accounts for the fact that most sales are made after the customer (victim) has said no at least two times for prize pitches and seven times in investment pitches. The seasoned pro knows that after pressing the money button, the next step is to give attention, to feed the ego of the victim, to make the victim feel special. Psychological manipulation at its best. Everyone wants to feel special and most of us do not feel we get the attention we should deserve. The frauder will ask personal questions, the favorites being, "What line of work are you in?" "What did you do before you retired?" "How did you get into something like that?" or "You sound like a pretty smart guy (gal), you sound like you have done pretty good for yourself." "I got lucky, I made my big money in the gold and silver run, in 1980. Did you take advantage of that one? Let me ask you, what was your first investment?"

One common characteristic among the victims in these stories is that their first instinct was to like and trust the frauder. Realizing this will help you to spot and defeat these victimizers of Americans. Whenever someone you do not know contacts you to pitch you about anything, do not allow yourself to open up to that person. Examine the facts.

The frauder may have information about you before contacting you. In this 'information age' we live in there are ways of purchasing information lists. These lists can be as specific as to tell how long you have lived at your address, your marital status, what credit cards you have, your families names and ages, your bank account information plus more.

If you are one of those rare individuals who has no additional financial goals, one who accepts life as it is and has no personal problems you are not a target.

If you are like the rest of us, you may be taken. Many of John T.'s favorite clients were professionals who thought they could never be taken. That was their weak point.

There is no personality profile that would make one safe from being victimized by a confidence person. Everyone is eligible to participate in these schemes. You decrease your odds tremendously by being aware of the problem, knowledgeable about their approaches, and active in helping law enforcement solve these problems.

RICHARD ROGERS

Richard Rogers was a con man operating during the early and mid-1980s. His business was selling siding and storm windows to seniors. The prices for his services varied widely, usually depending on what the market would bare; in other words, how much money the victim had.

Very few of Rogers' customers received competent service and most paid thousands of dollars in advance only to have less than half or none of the work completed. Rogers was a classic con man who preyed on loneliness, especially among older adults.

Donna Prudesky worked for Mr. Rogers for approximately six months and provided us with an inside perspective of how he targeted seniors—especially lonely ones. She testified in the case the attorney general's office brought against Mr. Rogers that she was hired to secure leads. She was told to look up names in the phone book that looked like older names: George and Hazel Smitherton, or Henry and Henrietta Anderson. She would call and suggest that their company, Allied Construction, was having a 50 percent off sale on storm windows and they would be willing to send a sales consultant out to the customer's house at no obligation to provide an estimate.

Depending on how the person responded to this pitch, she would make notations on a three by five inch lead card. Rogers instructed her not only to schedule appointments, but also to indicate whether the "customer" lived alone, sounded lonely, or was very talkative. These are the leads to which he would immediately respond.

The scam was simple: convince an elderly woman (or man) that she would save a fortune on her heating bills next winter by having Rogers install customized double-insulated thermopane windows on her mobile home. Rogers would always tell the consumer that his suppliers did business the old-fashioned way: they demanded payment in full up front on all supplies. Therefore, he required the customer to pay for the entire job in advance as well.

Rogers would always send a crew out the very next day after collecting the $3,000 or $4,000 check for the entire job. The reason he did this is to elude the police. The crew would go out to the site for about a half day—just long enough to make it impossible for a prosecutor to prove he took the money up front with *no intention* of doing the work.

The job would never be completed and, when confronted, Rogers would say that he fully intended to finish the job but he started having business problems or he caught one of his employees embezzling money and he was going to have to file bankruptcy.

This excuse could be used once or twice, but Rogers had collected money from over fifty people in a six-month period and finished only half a dozen jobs. The others were all the same story: Rogers immediately began work, then disappeared never to return.

Donna testified that one time she handed Rogers a lead which indicated the person was a lonely, elderly widow. Rogers took the lead, smiled and said, "I think Hazel could use some company. Maybe I'll call her back right now and say we had a cancellation and I can come out today."

It is not surprising that the vast majority of Rogers' victims were seniors. Also, not surprisingly, when I interviewed these victims, almost without exception, they were defensive of Rogers, stating, "I can't believe such a nice man could do a thing like this." Many of them said he was willing to spend time with them and some even fed him meals.

Rogers was eventually compelled by the state to return the thousands of dollars he had taken from senior consumers. This occurred however only after three investigators spent eight straight days on a massive man hunt to catch Rogers and serve court documents on him. Apparently, once he knew his employee had "spilled the beans" he skipped town in a hurry.

I sometimes felt as a fraud investigator that I spent more time trying to serve defendants than actually investigating them. This was definitely the case with Rogers. At one point in the hunt for this flimflam man, I remember coming up with what I thought was a particularly creative solution. It was right around Valentine's Day when we were looking for him. He and his wife had been holed up in a trailer in a rural part of Shelton, Washington.

I had staked out the trailer for days and I knew they were using it because cars changed parking spots, lights went on and off, and I could hear people inside. But they refused to answer the door. So I got the bright idea to send Mrs. Rogers a Valentine present: a box of chocolates with the lawsuit's pleadings hidden inside. I figured she would accept the chocolate and sign for it, thinking it was a gift from one of her con artist buddies, then open it and find that she had been served.

So I bought the chocolate and one of my volunteers convinced me to remove the chocolate (why reward con artists?) and replace them with little tiny rocks so the box would weigh roughly the same. Then I carefully placed the legal pleadings underneath the individually wrapped rocks and had an overnight express delivery runner deliver them. As clever as I thought this was, Mrs. Rogers' instincts were better than expected and she refused the package.

After an exhaustive hunt which included an eighty-five-hour stakeout of an apartment which Rogers used and a private mailbox where he had his mail sent, we caught him going in to see his lawyer in a downtown Seattle office building.

Rogers' lawyer decided to settle with us since our civil action was apparently less problematic than the IRS problems Rogers had gotten himself into. He agreed to pay back all of the consumers over about a thirty-six-month period. I can tell you however that—true to form—after making restitution payments for about six months, he stopped sending them and we never collected the rest of the money owed.

Lessons Learned

If you are concerned that you need work done on you house, look up three contractors in the yellow pages and get competitive bids from each of them. Make sure the contractor you hire is licensed and bonded. Check with the contractor's bonding company prior to hiring him to find out if any claims have been made against the bond. This can usually be done by calling the contractor registration division of the Department of Labor. If you are in doubt about where to call, the attorney general's office will be able to refer you to the proper agency.

Remember, if someone knocks on your door or, in Rogers' case, someone calls you and wants to make an appointment to come out to your house, be wary. You are much more in control when you initiate contact with the contractor. Most of the contractor complaints I saw in the attorney general's office were the result of the contractor selling the customer in his or her home, collecting the money in advance of performing any services, then failing to complete the work or doing a shoddy job.

One final point about contractors: It is advisable to pay them as they complete work on your home. For example, you can tell them you want to pay them 25 percent down, then when 25 percent of the work is finished, you will pay them another 25 percent, and so on until the work is finished.

We have had problems in the past with consumers who pay the contractor off in full. The contractor completes the work and everything is fine until one of the subcontractors places a workman's lien on the house claiming the general contractor failed to pay him. This can cloud your title and prevent you from selling or refinancing your home until you clear it up.

By paying the general contractor on a "pay as you go" basis and asking for evidence that subcontractors have been paid, you minimize the risk of this happening.

MUSIC LIBRARY

In the early 1980s, a company called Music Library came into the state of Washington and began a telemarketing operation in Seattle, Tacoma, and Olympia. In each of these three cities, the local Music Library "franchise" went by a different name. The product was cassette tapes which you could select from a catalog that supposedly had any title a person could want from rock to jazz, from Mozart to the Rolling Stones.

The local franchisees set up their own telemarketing operations, but everything was really controlled by the franchiser located in Huntington Beach, California. The telemarketer would convince consumers to sit through the in-home presentation by promising them a free cassette recorder worth over $100.

Once in the home, the presenter had a rather hokey pitch which included selling the virtues of cassettes over other types of music formats. He would pull out a badly warped record album and say, "Has this ever happened to you? You accidentally put a record on the couch, the sun shines on it for a couple of hours and that's it."

Then he would pull out a reel to reel tape that had been badly unraveled and say, "What about this mess, look familiar? I thought so."

After trashing the various other music formats, he would then say that the Music Library catalog had cassette tapes of the latest music on the market as well as titles from the 1950s and 1960s. The deal was as follows: The consumer entered into an agreement to buy one hundred tapes for $7.95 a piece or $795, financed over 36 months at $26.41 per month. This enabled the consumer to select any tapes he or she wished from the Music Library catalog in the convenience of the home, mail in the orders for up to one hundred tapes over the next three years, and have them shipped directly to his or her home.

What the presenter didn't say is that Music Library's catalog contained only what the music industry refers to as "cut-outs," titles which for one reason or another have not sold or were overproduced. These are the tapes you can buy in music stores for anywhere from ninety-nine cents to $4.99. Furthermore, the attorney general's investigation later revealed that the company president was being investigated by the Recording Industry Association of America and the FBI for unauthorized reproduction of copyrighted music.

Upon further investigation, we discovered that this company had been chased out of California and several other states and had come to Washington to operate as long as they could before we chased them out.

It was just a fluke however that we found this information because then, as now, there was no consistent information-sharing between states about fraud cases. I will say that I quickly learned as an investigator that when a new scam arrived in Washington, it probably came from either California or Nevada.

This was a classic case of a company which was very mobile and which tried to wrap the cloak of legitimacy around its operation. It was similar to Richard Rogers going out to the job site and starting the job, only to leave most of it unfinished. If you deliver something—anything—to the consumer, the police and prosecutors won't touch it. In this example, consumers were prepaying the full retail list price for one hundred tapes, only to find out the only tapes they could order were worth less than half the retail price. But they did get tapes—it's just that they were grossly overpriced.

We learned after driving the company out of Washington that it simply moved to another state. Also, even though we named the franchisees who were running the operation locally, they had no assets to attach and the owner of Music Library blamed the sales abuses on the franchisees, thereby distancing himself from criminal liability. It is a common tactic to simply cut off the infected arm of the octopus the minute trouble arises, thereby preserving the main part of the operation: the brain.

Lessons Learned

You should always demand complete information about the product before making a buying decision. If victims of the Music Library scam had demanded to see the catalog before buying, they would have realized that they had only "cut-outs" and older music available, yet they were paying current market value for it.

In-home presentations sometimes make people hesitant to ask for more information because the person has come all the way out to your house. Throw in a free cassette recorder and some people feel obligated to buy. This is obviously a mistake.

As much as it sounds convenient for a salesperson to come out to your house, I strongly discourage it. This book has discussed numerous scams that involve in-home presentations to older consumers which result in victimization.

Ironically, I believe consumers are more in control when they initiate contact and go to the business' store. This gives you the option to walk out since the business didn't go out of its way to meet with you the way it implicitly does in your home. Also, there are often other people around in a store so the salesperson can't isolate and badger the customer as easily.

If you do find yourself with a salesperson in your home, do not make a buying decision on the spot. Tell the salesperson you have a personal rule that says you always give yourself at least twenty-four hours before you decide to buy something—period. There is no deal out there that can't wait twenty-four hours for you to think it over. If the salesperson says it's a one-time deal only and you have to decide immediately, tell him you've decided not to buy.

MARK BAILEY

The most complex case I ever worked on was the Desert Investments (D.I.) case from 1985 to 1986. It is a good example of wrapping the "cloak of legitimacy" around a fraud operation and it demonstrates just how difficult it can be to prosecute con artists.

This company operated in Vancouver, Washington. It sold deed of trust investments primarily to seniors. The firm offered returns of between 18 to 21 percent secured by real estate. This rate was attractive to investors because it was 8 to 11 percent above normal interest rates at the time. The owners, Mark Bailey and Emily Richardson, had purchased a property management company by the same name which had been in business in the Vancouver area for over twenty years. This gave them instant credibility within the community. They kept the management company, but used the long-standing credibility of the firm to expand into the selling of investments.

The scheme was enormously complex. They created a company called Martin-Lee (which was a conjunction of their respective middle names) that was to become the holding company for the purchase of real estate. They would make an offer to buy a home for $50,000, then make the sale contingent upon their appraiser appraising the house for $80,000 to $90,000. We later learned that the appraiser would appraise these homes for whatever value Desert Investments wished. D.I. then purchased the home for $50,000 and assumed a mortgage of $30,000.

With the appraisal in hand, they would create a $10,000 note at 18 percent interest between Martin-Lee and D.I., with D.I. as lender and Martin-Lee as borrower. The note was secured by a second deed of trust on the property. Once they structured such a deal, they would go to an investor and tell him that D.I. wished to sell its interest in the second deed of trust. They told him that for $10,000, they could receive an 18 percent return which was "fully secured" by a home worth $90,000. And since the only other debt on the property was a $30,000 first mortgage, if anything went wrong, there was $50,000 in equity to fall back on (the $90,000 house minus a total of $40,000 in debt).

What they failed to tell consumers is that the house was really only worth $50,000. They also failed to tell them that they had created two more $10,000 notes secured by the same property and that the house worth $50,000 now had $60,000 worth of debt on it. The other two notes were also created and sold to investors, with no one investor being made aware of the other.

This scheme allowed Bailey and Richardson to generate huge amounts of cash each time they closed a home. They rented the homes and started making interest-only payments to the investors which satisfied them for close to two years. In this sense, it was a classic Ponzi scheme: robbing Peter to pay Paul.

They had so many investors interested solely due to the high returns that they were able to accumulate over one hundred homes during a two-year period valued at over $7 million! Over five hundred investors coughed up $3.5 million during this time.

The most frustrating aspect of this case was that they had successfully convinced all five hundred investors that it was a perfectly legitimate investment, even though they lied to every single victim about the value of the house securing the investment. For months, investors refused to talk to me because they were convinced there was nothing wrong, especially since they continued to receive their monthly payments.

Bailey was also telling them that the only thing threatening their investments was the state of Washington which was on a witch hunt to close down an otherwise perfectly legitimate business.

Eventually, I was able to interview some of the victims and one interview I did just before we sued them stands out in my mind. The woman, Mrs. Ethyl Johnson, lived with her husband Harold in a modest home just outside of Vancouver.

Mrs. Johnson had been attracted to Desert Investments because they advertised 18 percent returns on fully-secured real estate investments.

When they went in to Desert, they were shown a $25,000 note secured by a $135,000 home. There was $80,000 in existing debt on it which gave her enough equity to feel secure ($105,000 in total debt secured by a $135,000 house), so she gave them a check for $25,000.

When I looked up the title documents on this house, I found that Bailey and Richardson had bought the house for $50,000 six months before and had created three phony notes worth $10,000 each on it.

They had gotten a phony appraisal on the home saying it was worth $105,000 and then, in order to borrow more money from investors like Mrs. Johnson, they created a fake sale to a straw, or fake, buyer named Jessie Anderson (one of their employees) for $135,000. This transaction was on paper only and later Anderson testified that he often would simply sign blank documents, not even knowing what they were for.

The bottom line for Mrs. Johnson was that she had a note secured by a $50,000 piece of property that already had $80,000 in debt on it which meant she wasn't secured by the property at all! That is why I wanted to interview her that day; she was one of Desert's worst victims.

Bailey and Richardson were furious that I was talking to their investors and when I arrived at Mrs. Johnson's home, Emily Richardson and her attorney were there waiting for me. Mrs. Johnson had called Richardson to ask why a state investigator wanted to talk to her and Richardson said she didn't know, but asked if she could come and listen.

When I sat down, I noticed that Richardson had a gold cross hanging around her neck and she was sitting close to Mrs. Johnson with her hand on her arm. She said to Mrs. Johnson, "Now you know we have your best interest at heart here and we would never do anything to hurt you." I couldn't believe she stooped so low! Here she had swindled this poor woman's life savings and she had the audacity to express concern about her well-being.

I knew I couldn't conduct the interview with the attorney and future defendant present, so I indicated that to Mrs. Johnson. At that point her attorney said, "Mrs. Johnson has been gracious enough to invite us into her home and we are going to stay here until she tells us to leave." I said, "Well, you can sit here all day if you want to, but I am not going to conduct an interview under these circumstances." As I got up to leave, Mrs. Johnson told them they had better leave, which they did. I then interviewed Mrs. Johnson and got her to sign an affidavit for use against D.I.

I was so infuriated by this that I immediately went back to the office, told the attorney that we had enough information, and the next week visited Ms. Richardson, gold cross and all. As the police arrived to serve her, she was just pulling into the driveway of her new home on the golf course in a brand new Jeep truck (all paid for with the life savings of her victims).

As she got out of the truck, I went up to her and in front of her friends, I handed her 137 pages of legal pleadings naming her as defendant, and said, "Last week at Mrs. Johnson's home, you seemed to have a number of questions about our investigation. I think these documents will answer most of those questions."

The outcome of that case was not nearly as pleasing as that moment when I had finally given the con artist her due. The company immediately hid all of the documents, filed bankruptcy, and because the properties had been so overencumbered, the investors received about ten cents on the dollar. No 18 percent interest, no apologies from the company, and, for many of the investors, it meant the loss of their life savings.

Even more infuriating to me was the fact that within two weeks after filing bankruptcy, Mark Bailey moved ten miles south to Portland, Oregon, and started a new investment company! From that moment forward, I have been absolutely dedicated to the notion that more efforts should be made at educating consumers about fraud. I spent 2,400 hours of my life closing down a business which stole $3.5 million from five hundred seniors and within two weeks they were back in business ten miles away.

When we went to the local prosecuting attorney's office with the case, he simply shrugged his shoulders in bewilderment and said that if he tried to prosecute such a big case, he couldn't file anything else for a year.

There is some justice in the world, however. We did hand the case over to the FBI in 1988. Sixty-five boxes of documents were made available to the U.S. Attorney in Seattle in what had become one of the largest consumer protection cases we filed in the 1980s.

In 1992, some six years after we filed civil charges against Mark Bailey and Emily Richardson, they were indicted by a federal grand jury on forty-one counts of wire and mail fraud. Bailey was sentenced to five years in prison, a sentence he is currently serving. Richardson turned state's evidence against Bailey and was given a suspended sentence.

Lessons Learned
1. Don't be duped by high-yielding investments.

The old expression, "If you chase rate, you chase risk" certainly applies here. The victims of Desert Investments were so intent on getting 18 to 21 percent returns that they let down their guard and trusted a con artist who took their money.

2. Have an attorney review all documents before making large investment decisions.

If the victims of Desert had first had their attorney review the documents, they would have never invested to begin with. Always have your attorney review any investments before deciding to invest.

THE TRANSIENT PAVERS

In the fall of 1987 a group of traveling con artists hit the small town of South Bend, Washington. Unlike telemarketing fraud operators, these individuals came into South Bend to pull the classic door-to-door home improvement scam.

The approach was to drive around this rural town in new, leased trucks with hot blacktop in tow. The scamsters would look for homes which had older adults in the yard and which had gravel or dirt driveways. The pitch was to pull up, go over to the person living in the house, and say:

"Hi there. I was just doing a paving job down the street and I had some material left over. Now as you must know, hot blacktop won't keep and I ordered too much. Now I am willing to give you a great deal. I'll blacktop your driveway for you and only charge you for materials, no labor charge. How is that for a great deal?"

Sounds like a simple pitch, right? It is simple. But the eighty-seven-year-old man named Chester who was this group's first victim had quite a surprise coming when the con artist finished the job. They had laid a patch of blacktop approximately ten feet wide by twenty-five feet long and about a half-inch thick. The layer was so thin that within two weeks, there was grass growing up through the pavement. When the two principals of "Gary's Paving" encountered mild resistance from this frail old man, they grabbed his checkbook from him, filled out the amount of $4,500, and forced him to sign it.

Chester complained to the local sheriff's office and Detective Rick Benson was assigned the case. When he began to investigate, he found that this group had hit six other older adults in the area during a one-week period. Detective Benson was absolutely incensed at these cases which almost without exception involved the pitch just described, outrageous bills, and incomplete or shoddy workmanship. Benson was able to confront them on one occasion and threatened to put them in jail if they didn't leave town.

The basis for his threat was a technical violation of the city licensing law which they had violated by not purchasing a permit to solicit within the city limits of South Bend. Because the schemers had performed a service, albeit a shoddy one, he was unable to arrest them for theft or fraud. At this point he contacted the state attorney general's office in hopes that we could at least prosecute them civilly. Unfortunately, his pressure had forced them to leave for another town and another set of victims.

I had numerous experiences with these so-called "gypsy" operators and, almost without exception, we had succeeded in scaring them out of town or out of the state, but we never were able to serve papers, prosecute, or get the consumer's money back because they instinctively knew when the heat was too great.

This time was different however. We had a new, young aggressive assistant attorney general who was willing to pursue any bad guy he heard about and do it fast. So we drafted a complaint and went about the business of trying to find these characters to serve them.

This began a three-month-long chase which began in South Bend and ended up in Phoenix, Arizona. During this period of time, we were able to track where the gypsies went because each time they entered a new town with their caravan of new trucks and travel trailers, they would enroll their children in the local school. Detective Benson was able to work with the local South Bend school district who was contacted first by a district in Eugene, requesting records for the children who now attended school in Oregon.

As soon as we learned of this, we mobilized sheriff detectives in the area to look for and serve the defendants whom Benson had taken pictures of while they were being questioned in South Bend. Unfortunately, the pavers got wind of this when they saw the sheriffs approaching. They denied they were the defendants and before the sheriff could get more identifying information on them from us, they left town.

The next town they went to was Medford, Oregon, and once again they enrolled their kids in the local school. We had informed the Eugene School District to let us know if information about these same children was requested in the near future and if so, from whom. Thus we were able to send documents and identifying information to the Medford authorities, but again, the pavers eluded us.

As we chased these people down the West Coast, I recall setting up a map in my office which had a red line going down the coast line. This map represented our intense efforts to finally bust these transient gypsy scam artists. After fruitless attempts in Eugene, Medford, and Redding, California, we were finally able to serve these people in Phoenix.

They were headed there for the winter because it is hard to run a blacktop paving scam in the Pacific Northwest during the rainy winter months and also because the "snowbirds" all converged in Phoenix in the winter. "Snowbirds," of course, is the affectionate name for seniors from all over the north country who head south for the winter to bask in the warm Phoenix sunshine. The combination of guaranteed sunshine and thousands of seniors makes Phoenix an ideal winter location for gypsy con artists.

The unfortunate ending to this story is that it was simply impractical for us to prosecute "Gary's Paving" from another state. After our creative, valiant, and quite irregular efforts to serve these people, we never were able to get the victims' money back. And for eighty-seven-year-old Chester who lost his life savings, an A for effort didn't mean much.

Lessons Learned

The simple rule for avoiding this type of fraud scheme is: Never hire a contractor unless you have contacted him from ads in the yellow pages and he is licensed and bonded.

Any time a person knocks on your door and says he is a paver or a roofer, you should tell him you're not interested—period. It is important for you to know that con artists are typically nonviolent people. Therefore, if you turn away a door-to-door roofer who in fact is a con artist trying to victimize you, there is little chance he will physically threaten you.

The reason is simple: he knows if he beats someone up, the police will be called and he will be arrested and the bail will be expensive. On the other hand, if you turn him away, he knows there is always some poor guy down the street who *will* fall for his pitch—hook, line, and sinker.

WILLIAM CANON

The sweepstakes mentality was the catalyst for another scheme during the 1980s which targeted older consumers. It was called Master Investments, Inc. and was probably the most ingenious fraud scheme I have ever encountered.

The victims of this scheme saw it as an opportunity to draw supplemental income without having to risk any "new" capital.

The Master Investments company offered investment opportunities based on the investment tax credit law which was in effect at that time. The investment tax credit law was passed to provide incentives to businesses to recapitalize their operations. The law said if you purchase new capital, whether it be a building, a new tractor, or whatever, you can claim 10 percent of the purchase price as a tax credit on that year's taxes.

The law also said that if you purchased new equipment, then leased it to a third party, you could pass through the tax credit benefit to that third party.

The founder of this scheme, William Canon, claimed to have master recordings of famous artist's music such as Waylon Jennings, Elvis Presley, and Johnny Cash. These master recordings were available for lease so that individuals could go into the business of making albums from the master recordings, then sell them to record stores.

The pitch to individual consumers was as follows: We have a master recording of Elvis Presley's "Jail House Rock" which is valued at $600,000. The value of the master was based on what Master Investments had paid for it. Under the investment tax credit law, if you lease this master recording, Master Investments will allow you to claim the investment tax credit benefit, thus enabling the investor to claim a tax credit of 10 percent of the master's value or $60,000.

Now you may wonder why a retired person who earns about $30,000 per year and pays no more than $4,000 or $5,000 per year in taxes would need a $60,000 tax credit? You may also wonder how retired people could make the lease payments on such an expensive product. Well, the people at Master Investments had that all worked out.

Master Investments claimed to have an accountant who used to work for the Internal Revenue Service and understood all of the inner workings of the IRS. This person would meet with a group of prospective investors and find out how much each of them had paid in taxes over the previous three-year period. For this particular group, let's say the average prospect had paid $5,000 per year in taxes or $15,000 over three years.

Under the investment tax credit rules at that time, if you could show that you were leasing a newly purchased piece of equipment and the owner was willing to pass through the investment tax credit, you could retroactively amend your previous three year's taxes and, within forty-five days, the IRS was required to send you a refund reflecting the tax credit!

So Master Investments would take four older consumers, sign them up to lease a master recording of "Benny Goodman's Greatest Hits," which had just been purchased for $600,000. They would each receive 25 percent of the lease and therefore be eligible for 25 percent of the $60,000 tax credit. The accountant would then retroactively amend each of the consumer's tax returns for the previous three years and forty-five days later, each received a check from the IRS for $15,000.

You're probably wondering how much of that $15,000 they had to spend on the leasing of the master recording? Usually the lease was for ninety-nine years and consumers paid a one-time lease fee. The amount almost always was just under the refund amount. So to lease the $600,000 master of "Jail House Rock" cost the four investors around $55,000 collectively or $13,750 a piece.

So you can see the beauty of this operation. Master Investments, in effect, helped the investor create the investment money which he or she needed to go into the business of making records. The risk to the investor wasn't very great because even if he or she never made a single record, it was money the investor had given to the government anyway.

The outcome of this investment however was catastrophic for the five hundred or so older adults who fell for it. About three years after most of the investors signed up, the IRS declared the Master Investments master recording offer to be a fraudulent and abusive tax shelter.

The IRS investigation revealed the same thing the attorney general's did. The values of the master recordings had been grossly inflated via numerous fake transactions between fictitious companies. We did title histories which showed that the Benny Goodman master was really a bootleg recording that was initially purchased for $1,000 (without the authorization of the artist). The next day it was purchased for $50,000, followed by another sale the next week for $100,000. Finally, it was sold days after that to Master Investments for the represented value of $600,000.

Master Investments had done this with every single master recording which they marketed via the investment tax credit plan.

The real tragedy of this case was that the mastermind, William Canon, left the country and put the millions he had made in banks in the Grand Cayman Islands so the IRS could not get the funds. The individual taxpayers were left having to repay the money.

The IRS sent notices to all five hundred investors denying the shelter and demanding that they return the money they received from the tax refunds orchestrated by Master Investments' accountants. But since most of the refund money had been spent on the ninety-nine-year leases which were collected up front as a condition of Master Investments passing through the investment tax credit, the victims had no ability to pay the money back.

The IRS then put liens on the homes of hundreds of older consumers for the amount of the claimed tax refunds orchestrated through Master Investments plus penalties as high as 30 percent for participating in an abusive tax shelter scheme.

When I interviewed the victims of this scam, many of them indicated that they had decided to do it because their friends had done it and because, as retirees, they needed to find a supplemental source of money. Also, they had been convinced by the Master Investments salespeople that the investors really had nothing to lose. Finally, they felt it was on the up and up because the company had hired an ex-IRS employee.

It is important to note the limitations of law enforcement here. The justice department indicted the operators of this fraudulent tax shelter, but never found any of the money as far as I am aware.

The victims of this scheme were primarily older consumers, and there were other investment tax credit schemes during the 1980s which marketed bull service and other exotic kinds of "new capital." The 1990s may very well see a new wave of such schemes as Congress considers bringing back the investment tax credit law. Don't be fooled again!

Lessons Learned

This scheme, although it may seem farfetched, does appeal to older persons on fixed incomes since it provides a way to start a business (in theory) without risking a lot of your own money. It is particularly attractive when interest rates are so low that seniors who live on interest income are searching for new sources of cash flow.

As with so many con games, the important thing to remember is that if it sounds too good to be true, it isn't true. Before messing around with your tax returns, be sure to get advice from your accountant or from an attorney who is familiar with IRS regulations.

All of the con artists profiled in this chapter had one thing in common: they were thieves pretending to be business people. I have worked over the years with many legitimate business people and they are among the most impressive individuals I know. Most businesses in America are run by tireless, honest folks who understand that treating consumers fairly and honestly is the best way to be successful and—yes—profitable.

The trick to avoiding fraud is to filter out the handful of crooks who are out for a quick buck by offering incredible deals from those who offer fair prices and good service. It is really quite simple to unveil the "cloak of legitimacy" which was discussed at the beginning of chapter 4 by using common sense.

Another theme outlined in chapter 4, the "sweepstakes mentality," is also worth mentioning again. American consumers seem to have an insatiable desire to win big prizes and get good deals. This desire is routinely exploited by con artists by emphasizing profits and ignoring the risks. In the case of Mark Bailey and Desert Investments, clearly the victims saw only the benefits of getting 20 percent returns and ignored the possibility that there might be risks associated with above market rates of interest. In the case of William Canon and Master Investments, the victims were told there was no risk because the money they were to invest was "created" by Canon's former IRS accountant in the form of retroactive tax refunds.

In the complex economy of the 1990s, it pays to operate conservatively, take your time (especially with investments), and, most importantly, do you homework on a firm before doing business with them.

CHAPTER

6

SECRETS OF THE TELEPHONE FRAUD TRADE: SCAMSTERS AT WORK

"How cheerfully he seems to grin, how neatly spreads his claws, and welcomes little fishes in the greatly smiling jaws."

—Lewis Carroll, from *Alice in Wonderland*

Telemarketing is a $400 billion business per year in the United States. There is no way to tell how much of it is fraudulent, but estimates indicate that it is in the tens of billions annually.

Congressional hearings held in 1991 estimate that older Americans lose at least $5 billion per year to telemarketing fraud. Testimony at those hearings from former boiler room con artists make it very clear who they liked to target.

"We targeted the wealthy and the elderly in our fraud. Retirees were easily accessible by phone, usually at home during the day, and thus easy to resell. We found the elderly intent on enlarging their nest egg, their limited income, and often interested in generating money for their grandchildren," said a former convicted con man at the hearings.

"The elderly are vulnerable because their memory is poor, they rarely memorialize phone conversation into writing, and only occasionally ask for written guarantees . . . Their most notable weakness is that once they recognize the deceit, they are often too embarrassed to relay the events to their children, friends, counsel, and law enforcement."

This testimony supports what you will hear John T. say in this chapter about the business. It also supports findings from the FBI in a recent nationwide sting called "Operation Disconnect." This undercover operation identified ninety-five illegal boiler rooms nationwide and over five hundred salespeople were arrested and charged in March 1993 with wire fraud and other counts.

The following interview with John T. reveals some of the strategy and psychology behind how these telemarketers swindle older persons and why they continue to be a favorite target for telephone con artists.

Following the interview are five fraud transcripts which were the result of tape-recorded reenactments between John and I over a six-month period during which I played the role of the victim and he would deliver his pitch just like he did in real life for over ten years. To my knowledge, these transcripts represent the first time that fraudulent sales scripts actually used by telephone con artists have been published for widespread distribution. For you, the reader, it is a rare opportunity to catch an inside glimpse of how it is done, word for word, in boiler rooms across the country.

AN INTERVIEW WITH ONE OF AMERICA'S MOST NOTORIOUS CON ARTISTS

DOUG: John, you've indicated that seniors are particularly vulnerable to fraud schemes like the ones you did throughout the 1980s. Why is that?

JOHN: The number one reason is that many seniors are lonely. If your friends have been passing away and you don't have anyone to go out and do things with, you're going to be lonely. So now, this telephone salesperson calls you up and tells you that you don't have to be lonely anymore because he will take care of you. All of a sudden the person at the other end of the phone is vulnerable.

DOUG: How did you go about finding seniors to exploit?

JOHN: The best targets actually are older women living alone. It is a statistical fact that there are many more senior women living alone than men. Women outlive men. And they are like sitting ducks for con artists.

Say I wanted to sell oil lease investments to a woman named Edie. Now I would get Edie's name from a lead company. These are firms which collect names of investors who have sent away for information in the past about one type of investment or another. So I know Edie is interested in investing.

The key to selling these ladies is to first become friends with them. I would often talk to a person several times on the phone before asking for the sale. During the initial conversations, I would find out about her life, listen to her stories, and basically keep her company. I would also use flattery to befriend her. I would say things like:

"Edie, you couldn't possibly be seventy-five years young. Why my wife is only thirty-five and you sound just like she does over the phone."

Once she is my friend and trusts me, I can sell her until she runs out of money to invest.

DOUG: Did the victims always invest or did you have some people who were skeptical and objected?

JOHN: Any good salesperson will tell you that he welcomes objections . . . that's where a good salesperson is at his best. Let me give you an example of a pitch I would use. Let's say Edie told me she was afraid to make an investment decision since her husband used to take care of the finances. I would say something like:

"Edie, I want you to know I understand how you feel. You're afraid. I understand that. Being afraid is natural. Everyone is afraid at some point in his life. Edie, I want to share something with you I haven't told anyone else before, not even my wife.

"When my wife was pregnant with our first child, the doctor told us there may be complications in delivery. Now I never let on to my wife, but I was really afraid. I know, I know, men aren't supposed to be afraid. But I was scared to death that something might happen to my beautiful wife and, worse still, to our unborn child. So I know what you're going through. But there's no reason to be afraid.

"That's what I'm here for. I am here to protect you and teach you all of those things you don't understand about the oil business."

DOUG: Does that really work?

JOHN: Let's put it this way, it paid for a vacation in the Bahamas every other month for a year and a half. I was taking in $250,000 a month at one point.

DOUG: Were these good investments?

JOHN: Well, we were telling investors they could make up to $1 million on their investment of $14,000 over five years and most of them made nothing. In fact, most of them lost their initial investment.

DOUG: Were there really oil wells, or did you make that up?

JOHN: There were wells. That's why I'm not still in jail. But they were shallow wells and only two of them ever struck oil. We figured it cost between $50,000 and $75,000 to drill and we sold over $1 million worth of lease options on each well. The whole key to avoiding criminal prosecution is to pretend to be a legitimate business.

DOUG: In other words, wrap the "cloak of legitimacy" around your fraud scheme.

JOHN: Exactly.

DOUG: Give me another pitch you used to sell seniors.

JOHN: Well I guess the most ruthless approach was to target Alzheimer's patients.

DOUG: How would you do that?

JOHN: I would start out as usual, buying a name from a lead company. Then I would talk to the person over a series of days, sometimes staying on the phone for hours at a time listening to the stories. The whole time the person was talking, I was writing down what he or she said.

The next day I would ask the person about a story he or she had mentioned the day before. If the person couldn't remember the story, then I knew he or she was forgetful. So the third day, I would call back and say:

"Bill, this is John—the well outside of Lubbuck just hit and you told me you were going to wire the $15,000 last night. Did you forget to go to the bank Bill?"

Nine times out of ten, the person would send me the money out of embarrassment. I was preying on the person's insecurity about remembering things. This strategy worked especially well on men whose ego was at stake.

I had one client whose wife called me begging me to stop calling her husband. I asked her, "You have a roof over your head don't you?" She said yes. "You have money left in the bank don't you?" She said yes. "So what are you complaining about?"

DOUG: How did you think up new pitches?

JOHN: A number of the pitches I did used news events as the "hook." So whenever we were sitting around in the phone room trying to think up a new pitch, I would open up the newspaper. If I saw a headline story like "Hurricane Strikes Florida Coastline," it would result in a new scheme.

DOUG: Like what?

JOHN: I would most likely start up a phony charitable solicitation pitch that would go something like:

"Mr. Douglas, this is John Daniels from the Dade County Disaster Relief Center. You must have seen the news reports of thousands of Floridians left homeless by Hurricane Ralph. We are leading a fund-raising drive to build emergency shelters for thousands of homeless families and their small children whose lives have been devastated by this catastrophic event. The response to this effort has been overwhelming. Can I count on your support today?"

DOUG: So you use the fact that there was an event which everyone has heard about as a way of validating your pitch?

JOHN: Right. It's the same way with the free prize pitches. The Las Vegas vacation certificate pitch works primarily because there are so many giveaway promotions going on that are legitimate like clearinghouse giveaways or state lotteries that consumers dream of the day they are told they have won. When I call and say, "Congratulations, you've won the grand prize," all I'm doing is fulfilling that consumer's fantasy, even though there is no prize and it's all a scam.

DOUG: Some say that the only people who fall for con games are those who are uneducated and/or unintelligent. Is that true?

JOHN: Hey, listen, my favorite people to rip off were doctors and lawyers and highly educated people. You know why? Because they think they know everything. You wouldn't believe what I could get them to talk themselves into. I think anyone in this country can be had by people like me on any given day.

If I was trying to sell a doctor, I would tell him about how my father was a doctor:

"Dr. Smith, I learned one thing growing up as a doctor's son and that is you guys do nothing but work. Am I right? Seventy-eighty-ninety hours a week. I work five days a week, six hours per day. I have a thirty-five-foot Bayliner and a slip on the ocean and I tell ya, I'm on that boat every single day."

I'm telling you, the longer I did this, the more convinced I became that greed is a universal Achilles' heel. If I can convince an investor that I have the "Midas touch" and can make him a fortune, then I got him. I don't care who they are.

DOUG: If you had to give seniors advice to help them avoid frauders, what would it be?

JOHN: The first thing is shop in your own backyard instead of over the phone. That way you have some recourse if you have a problem. Most of my clients didn't even know where I was calling from.

Second, ask a friend or relative for advice before making a buying decision. This gives you time to think about whether it's a good deal or not.

And finally, beware of overly friendly strangers. I ripped off seniors by becoming their friends first, then stealing from them once I had their trust. If you are lonely, get involved in your community. Don't wait for me to call.

■ ▪ ■ ▪ ■ ▪ ■ ▪ ■

This book has identified and describes dozens of fraud schemes used by con artists to steal money from vulnerable seniors. This chapter provides the reader a rare peek inside the telemarketing fraud boiler rooms in the United States to see exactly what is being said over phone lines by con artists.

The following transcripts are actual tape-recorded reenactments made by myself and John. I play the role of the victim, one that comes naturally to me having interviewed hundreds of fraud victims over the years. John of course plays the fraudulent telemarketer, a role he plays almost too well as you will see.

Very little editing has been done in order to give the reader an accurate sense of what it is like to have a con artist on the other end of the phone line.

THE COLLECTIBLES PITCH

In this pitch, John has identified a "mooch," an elderly widow who has been taken to the cleaners by his con artist colleagues during the past six months. His information is that she has spent about $250,000 during this time and has been labeled among the room operators as "tapped out."

John has decided that he can get one last hit on this victim. He has a bet with his buddies: he bets a weekend in the Bahamas that he can get at least $5,000 from her. His buddies take the bet, saying things like, "You can't get blood out of a turnip." John's response to them was, "Maybe you can't, but I can."

John begins to call the target, Mary, on the premise that she had filled out a lead card to learn about some oil investments. Over a period of weeks, it becomes clear that Mary has in fact become low on cash and is wary of giving money to anyone.

What he decides to do is to call her every day—or sometimes every other day— and just talk to her. He asks her a lot of questions about her family and her past in an attempt to get her to trust him. After a couple of weeks, he senses that she now looks forward to him calling. He has determined that she lives alone, is widowed, and spends most of her time at home watching television and waiting for the mail carrier to come.

The script you are about to read is the pitch John goes into once he feels Mary considers him to be a friend more than a salesman. He is going to go for one of the most ruthless scams out there. He actually talks her into selling some of her personal belongings by giving them to him "on consignment" so she can improve her cash position. In truth however, he is going to take all of her most valuable jewelry and artwork, sell it, and spend the profits on fast women and expensive sports cars.

JOHN: Gosh Mary, I really wish I could help you here. It sounds to me like you're about down to your last ounce of gold. God knows I wish you had some money to invest so I could help you here.

MARY: But can you help me get my money back?

JOHN: No I can't Mary, but. . .

MARY: I trusted them.

JOHN: I understand that. Believe me, of all people, I understand that and you know . . . I'm going to do something I normally don't do. Cause I'll tell you something Mary, you remind me of my grandmother.

MARY: But I don't know you that well.

JOHN: Well, and I don't know you real good right now. As time goes along Mary, you're going to find that I'm the guy to have in your corner.

MARY: Really?

JOHN: You betcha. I've got an option store, its an upper-crust jewelry store actually. You know with the guards and everything? Have you ever seen one of those?

MARY: Uh-huh. But what do you do?

JOHN: What I do is to help people liquidate assets.

MARY: But, I don't have any assets. I gave all of my money away.

JOHN: I understand that, OK? And as tough as it may be sometimes, sometimes we have to do what we have to do so that we can continue to live.

MARY: All I have is my social security. I have no other income.

JOHN: I understand that Mary. What would you say if I told you you wouldn't have to give me one penny, but I could get you thousands of dollars?

MARY: How?

JOHN: Let me tell you, I had a client last week. He was an elderly gentleman who walked in and said that he had just not invested wisely and he had lost his money. It turns out that he had a painting that he brought in. I got it appraised at $87,000, I auctioned it at $92,000 and I only kept 10 percent. We gave Walter the rest of the money. He needs it more than we do you know what I mean?

MARY: Well, yes but I don't know if I have anything quite that valuable. That's amazing. I do have some family heirlooms, but I am not sure I'm ready to part with them. They are personally important to me. I don't know that I'd want to sell them.

JOHN: Yes, I understand.

MARY: But I do have quite a few things. In fact, my husband Harold before he died accused me of being a pack rat if you can believe that. I just never throw anything away. My house is full of stuff now that I stop and think about it. I just don't know if any of it is valuable.

JOHN: You know you sound like my wife. If she saves one more thing Mary, I'm going to have to go rent a storage room. Can you believe that?

MARY: Ha, ha, ha, ha.

JOHN: I want a motorcycle. Do I get a motorcycle? Nooooooo!

MARY: Ha, ha, ha.

JOHN: I tell ya, you gals are tough sometimes.

MARY: We just want to remember the things that we've had in the past, that's all.

JOHN: I understand.

MARY: I mean those are the things that we remember with. So the thought that they would ever be worth money is mind-boggling.

JOHN: Well, I'll tell you what we can do here because you can't inspect an item over the phone. I mean, heck, if we had that new video conferencing, you could hold it up to the phone and show me. Well let me ask ya, do you ever come down here to Florida?

MARY: I do during the winters, of course, that's what a lot of us older folks do. Is that where you're calling from?

JOHN: That's right. I'm sure you know the area of my storefront. Do you know where the Biscayne Mall is?

MARY: Oh sure. I had a condo about two miles from there.

JOHN: Well heck then you might have even come in here.

MARY: What do you do?

JOHN: We liquidate collectable assets for people. So normally the way it works Mary. . . .

MARY: I don't know that I want to give you my belongings.

JOHN: Well, you're not giving anybody anything. Of course everything is fully insured. As a matter of fact we overinsure every item. But the way it works Mary, it's real simple. We have two full-time appraisers who appraise everything. As a matter of fact, we have access to the University of Miami Anthropology Department. And they have even been known to help us track down some very old collectibles.

I had a gal who had a family hand-me-down, it was a broach. Nothing real special about it. Well, it turns out that particular broach was worn by a lady in 1776.

MARY: Really?

JOHN: Oh yeah. That broach was auctioned off at $22,000. So what you might come across and this happens a lot Mary, is we may only find a couple of the items to be worth a great deal of money. And heck if you can get that much money for say just one or two items and keep everything else, then that way you've got the money that you deserve to have. Because Mary, I'll tell ya, you owe it to yourself to live your golden years in the style that you deserve.

MARY: Oh, well that's really nice of you to say, I've never had anyone say anything like that to me before.

JOHN: Heck, I don't know if I told you, but you remind me of my grandmother.

MARY: Really? Well, how old are you?

JOHN: I'm thirty-two.

MARY: You know my grandson is thirty-four, you are just about his age. So what do I have to do then? All I want is a little money. Like I told you before, I lost this money through some poor decisions. My husband had just died, and these people started calling me and I didn't know what I was doing. I lost some income from that and all I want to do is have a comfortable living. I don't want to sell everything I have, but I would like a comfortable living.

JOHN: Mary, let me ask you this. If you sent me in say a ring and that ring turned out to be worth $100,000, you're not going to get mad at me if we auction it, are you?

MARY: Well, I don't think so. I don't think I have anything that's worth that much.

JOHN: You never know Mary.

MARY: I don't think I would have anything that valuable. I do have several rings.

JOHN: The way we would work it right now Mary, is I am going to transfer you over to my front office gal. She's going to take down an inventory sheet of the items you think may be worth something.

Then what we're going to do is, I'm going to go through the item sheet. I have been doing this for a few years and I pretty well know the types of assets we can liquidate and get you the top dollar.

I'll then be getting back with you to review that. Now will you be in this evening?

MARY: Yes I will.

JOHN: What time do you go to bed nowadays?

MARY: I usually turn in at 9:00 P.M.

JOHN: Early to bed, early to rise. . . .

MARY: Well you know I'm getting on in years . . . I'm not as young as I once was.

JOHN: I don't know, heck, you sound pretty feisty to me.

MARY: You know, I have a thirty-four-year-old grandson.

JOHN: Well how many other grandchildren to you have?

MARY: I have three grandchildren.

JOHN: Great, Great. And one's a boy.

MARY: Right, two girls.

JOHN: And two girls. So how did they do? Did they land the right kind of guy?

MARY: Well, the granddaughters did pretty well. One is married to an IBM salesman. He's doing quite nice, he's in Peoria. The other one is in Albuquerque, New Mexico, and she's married to a grocery store manager. So I'm happy with them both. They're lovely.

JOHN: Sound's like you've done a good job.

MARY: Well I do the best I can. I'm just really upset though about this money that I lost and if I thought I could make it back I'd . . .

JOHN: No, no. Mary please, OK. If you ever get ready to invest in something, I don't know, I've had ladies that I've helped that were just in a temporary cash crunch and when their real estate went up and they filled up their rentals, then they'd be doing OK. Well they would call me and they'd say, "John, I want to invest in something, I want to earn that money back." And you know the first thing I'd tell them? I'd tell them no.

MARY: No?

JOHN: No. It's time to be a bit conservative here. So when you call me, I'm gonna tell you about the track records of the mutual funds and things like that because I'll tell you Mary, God bless you, I hope you've learned your lesson.

MARY: Well I have, I have. I am very concerned about this. You know, before my husband died, he handled all of this and so I admit that I wasn't quite as knowledgeable as I should have been and I trusted some people that I shouldn't have trusted.

JOHN: Well heck, maybe I can help you get on your feet here a little bit. But please, will you promise me . . . Mary, before we go any further, you've got to promise me that if you decide to invest in something, you'll call me and I'll give you my opinion and I'll tell you who to call who's reliable.

MARY: I appreciate that John. By the way, how did you get my number again?

JOHN: You had filled out a card in regards to collectibles. It was in *Harper's, Life,* and *Reader's Digest.*

MARY: Oh yes, that's right.

JOHN: Do you get *Reader's Digest?*

MARY: Yes.

JOHN: OK, then you've seen the ad. Alrighty, if you'll hang on one second here, I'm going to have my girl get that inventory from you. Her name is April and she's a real nice girl. We'll then run that through a special computerized program and then I'll get back with ya and tell you what I think our best shot is here.

MARY: Thank you very much.

JOHN: Now what time will you be home this evening?

MARY: I go to bed at 9:00 P.M. and I'll be home all night.

JOHN: All right. OK. Do you have any favorite TV shows?

MARY: Ha, ha . . . I watch "Cosby." He's on between 8:00 and 8:30.

JOHN: OK, well I'll be giving you a call then sometime around 8:30. God bless you, Mary. Hang on a second and I'll get April for you.

After we did this reenactment, I asked John to talk about some of the psychological tricks he used to sell this woman. Here is what he said:

"The main thing I wanted to do at the beginning was to sympathize with her about her prior losses. I wanted her to think that I was going to watch out for her and make sure nothing bad happened to her. I wanted her to think that the only reason I was calling was to help her out of a jam.

"I tried to establish my credibility by describing my store as 'upscale', one that had a lot of expensive stuff in it. This aspect is something Doug would call the 'cloak of legitimacy'. I just call it a good pitch.

"By citing examples of what some of my clients supposedly were able to sell for huge profits, I wanted to give her hope, that maybe she had a broach that was worth $22,000. I mean, heck, anything is possible, right?

"Finally, by saying things like, 'You remind me of my grandmother,' I was attempting to become her friend and make her think I was going to be as nice to her as her own grandson.

"As ruthless as this sounds, I have been to rooms in Florida and Texas that specialized in taking mooches who were dry—which means broke—and hitting them for their jewelry, their family heirlooms, anything that was available. You have to realize that these guys [telephone fraud operators] are just out of their minds. I'm not trying to make excuses for what they did or for what I did. I'm just saying that there is nothing they won't try if it brings in money."

According to John, these operators are still doing "business" in various locations around the United States.

Coming soon to a city near you.

THE LAS VEGAS VACATION PITCH

This is a pitch which John says has been around since 1977 in precisely the form you will see here and is still being used today. It is one of the most successful pitches ever devised despite its relative simplicity.

The pitch starts with the "sweepstakes mentality" theme by telling the prospect he has won a free trip. The whole goal of this pitch is to convince the victim that he is getting something for nothing. John is going to sell Tim a one-year supply of vitamins for $362 and make him think he is getting them for 50 percent off and getting around paying a hefty gift tax on the "free" vacation.

In reality, the vacation is nothing more than discount coupons and the travel department of the operation will make it so difficult for Tim to take advantage of them that he will eventually give up. The vitamins, which he paid $362 for, could be purchased at a retail outlet for under $100. How did John do it? See for yourself.

JOHN: Hello, is this Tim Ruckert?

TIM: Yes.

JOHN: John Rogers. Congratulations. You've won an all-expenses paid vacation for three days and two nights in Las Vegas, Nevada.

TIM: You're kidding me.

JOHN: No. Have you ever won anything major before?

TIM: Well I don't think so. And I don't even remember entering a contest?

JOHN: Well you have now. Congratulations. The private limousine will be picking you up at the airport—you and your guest. Now you're gonna have your choice of Caesar's Palace or Tropicana—you know if you're a high roller, or if you're like the rest of us—ha, ha—you'll probably want to stay at Vegas World or the Excaliber or maybe downtown. Now they give you a fabulous personal Las Vegas Limousine Tour. OK?

TIM: Is that right?

JOHN: That's right. And they'll even pull up to five different casinos, stop at the front door, open the door for you and you and the missus can go in and tour the casino.

TIM: You know all of this is funny because I don't even remember entering a contest and you're telling me I've won?

JOHN: You were probably automatically entered in something. Do you have any credit cards?

TIM: Well sure, I have credit cards.

JOHN: OK, well all the time the Visa and Mastercard and American Express people are entering you into sweepstakes and you don't even know it.

TIM: Is that right?

JOHN: Oh yeah.

TIM: So I won for real then?

JOHN: Oh yeah—it's a fact. Now if you come during the summertime, there is a fantastic Lake Mead tour in a glass-bottom boat.

TIM: A Lake Mead tour? Where's Lake Mead?

JOHN: Lake Mead is the largest manmade lake in the world. Now what happened is when they built the Hoover Dam—they built the Hoover Dam in the late 1800s did you know that Tim?

TIM: No, I didn't know that.

JOHN: Oh yeah. That's actually when the Colorado River was routed over. And what happened was the state of Nevada—you know there weren't actually too many people out here then—but there were a couple of small towns—so the state of Nevada bought the land and flooded the valley. But you know what Tim, they didn't tell everybody. . . .

TIM: You mean there were people there when they did this?

JOHN: That's right, that's right. Now there's this one ghost town that they called Goldstrike and there was actually a *gun battle* going on at the time they diverted the Colorado River.

TIM: You're kidding?

JOHN: No, no I'm not kidding. You and your wife are going to be able to go on a glass-bottom boat excursion over this ghost town. And you will actually see the bones of people who died. We're talking about horses—the skeletons of horses tied up outside—you remember like those old John Wayne movies where they used to tie the horses up?

TIM: Yes.

JOHN: It is simply phenomenal.

TIM: Sounds like it. I have never really been down there before now that you mention it, so I don't really know much about that area. You're telling me you can actually take a glass-bottom boat out and see old Western towns?

JOHN: It's great, it's great. Now all of your meals are paid for—you can either have private meals or the buffet. Plus $500 to gamble with—now you have to gamble that at least once, wherever you stay, after all it's Vegas. Now you're also going to have your choice of shows for Saturday night—you know Tim, it's not like the old days when you had to pay a maitre'd $100 to sit in front. The casinos all do this through ticket agencies now.

TIM: Oh, I see.

JOHN: So you're guaranteed front-row seats at the casino show of your choice.

TIM: That's part of the deal?

JOHN: The agency does require that you make your reservations at least two weeks in advance, alrighty?

TIM: OK.

JOHN: Now when do you think you'll be able to take this vacation?

TIM: Well it's kind of the middle of the winter now, I guess I'd like to get away sometime in March?

JOHN: OK great, great. Well you'll be dealing with the travel agency and that's the Scamco Too Travel Agency. Now, like I said Tim, you are guaranteed this vacation no matter what. And as you said, you hadn't personally entered any sweepstakes or purchased anything.

TIM: Not that I can remember. Now my memory could be faulty.

JOHN: No, no I believe you. Ha, ha, ha.

TIM: You know I'm getting a little older and I don't remember things as well as I used to.

JOHN: Tim, you'd be surprised—you know my mom, she says she thinks she's getting Alzheimer's and she forgets and this and that—so what I did was I had her make a list of everything she forgot in the past week and I made a list of everything I forgot and you know what? I forgot more than she did. The thing is that when you get older, it's almost like people expect you to forget things and it becomes almost a self-fulfilling prophecy.

TIM: Well I know I worry about it because I have filled out things before and sometimes they come back to haunt me and I hope this isn't one of those things. I mean it sounds great because I'm winning and everything, but . . . I get nervous. I don't really know who you are for example.

JOHN: OK, well you're going to be receiving your official confirmation in writing on this, OK? And be my guest—you can check on us. Scamco is the authorized promotional agency for the sweepstakes. So you'll have a list of all the agencies and the numbers if you want to double check it cause I mean—people just aren't as honest as they used to be. But you won the vacation—congratulations!

TIM: You sound kind of honest.

JOHN: Why, thank you. You know my dad always told me a man's only as good as his word. If a man's word is no good, then the man's no good—it's that simple. And that's always stuck with me.

TIM: Well, what do I have to do?

JOHN: No, you don't have to do anything. You won the vacation. Now this is how it works. You know as well as I do that there's a gift tax. You know like if you won something on "Let's Make a Deal" or "The Price Is Right" or "Wheel of Fortune"?

TIM: Uh, huh.

JOHN: When you win something, the government wants 55 percent of that product's actual retail value. Now the products are always inflated about 25 percent because that's how the sponsors for the sweepstakes make their money. Are you with me so far?

TIM: I think so.

JOHN: Good. Now, what happens then is when you receive the vacation, you're also going to be receiving a tax form. And you're going to have to fill that tax form out and everything and they've got the vacation's retail value at $2,482.

TIM: Wow, I just won that much, huh?

JOHN: It's a fact—you know I had a cousin of mine, she won a car on "The Price Is Right"? And Dina and Gil had to sell the car because they couldn't afford to pay the taxes.

TIM: Is that right? You know I watch those shows every day and you see those happy faces—maybe later they're not so happy.

JOHN: There is no such thing as a free lunch.

TIM: I guess that's right.

JOHN: Now there is something we can do. And I want you to know it's totally up to you. No matter what, you've won the vacation. Alright, we've got another sponsor who has a complete line of vitamins. Now these vitamins—you've probably heard a lot of talk about the smart drinks—have you read about that in *Time* and *Newsweek?*

TIM: Yeah, where you can drink something and it will improve your memory or something like that?

JOHN: Exactly. Exactly. Now you get the Smart Drink powder formula along with one year's supply of top quality vitamins—vitamins A, B, C, D, Q—you know everything and also it has the essential minerals. Alrighty, these are top-of-the-line vitamins—they're Scamco vitamins. I'm sure you can walk into any mall or health food store and they'll tell you about them. Now, what we can do is we can get you a one-year supply of these Scamco vitamins and I can get those to you at a distributor cost, not the retail cost. So let me see here . . . that would be $362.

TIM: $362, huh?

JOHN: Right.

TIM: Well what are they normally worth?

JOHN: These vitamins and the Smart Drink powder formula? This is top-of-the-line stuff. This is scientific vitamins made from the latest neurological studies. So you are looking at a retail price on that in the stores of $5.00 per package . . . and that's for one day.

TIM: Oh and this is for a whole year, huh? I suppose I could do the math on that.

JOHN: Right. I'm sure you can probably find a one-year supply for around $700 if you got it mail order or something.

TIM: So your price is 50 percent off?

JOHN: Oh yeah. We're not here to make any money on this. Basically, we like to keep everything going and we like to utilize people in our advertising, OK?

Now what has happened in the past is when people find out about the taxes, they're still happy that they won something, but heck, the excitement's worn off a little bit and now they've got to pay a tax on it. So it's really hard to get a genuine smile.

So if you buy the vitamins, we'll include the vacation as a sales premium and you won't have to pay the gift tax on it. Also, what we want you to do, are you married?

TIM: Yes.

JOHN: What's your wife's name?

TIM: Martha.

JOHN: OK. We want you to have Martha take a picture of you pouring some of the power into the glass for that Smart Drink, OK?

TIM: OK.

JOHN: Now can you get your hands on a 35 millimeter camera? It has to be a 35 millimeter picture.

TIM: I can do that, but what would this be used for?

JOHN: It's going to be used in sweepstakes promotions and there is going to be a picture of you pouring that drink. Isn't that great! They're going to make you a star! Ha, ha, ha. Great, are you going to be home tomorrow?

TIM: Yes.

JOHN: OK. What I'll do is I'll have an overnight express delivery runner stop by um . . . grab a pen and a piece of paper—I'll hang on.

TIM: OK. Martha, can you get me a pen and some paper—just a minute now. OK, I'm ready, I've got a pen.

JOHN: That's Scamco Promotions.

TIM: Scamco Promotions.

JOHN: The address is 111 Scamco Lane, Las Vegas, Nevada. And the zip is 12345. OK now write down my name. My name is John Daniels. That's D-A-N-I-E-L-S.

TIM: Daniels.

JOHN: And the number you can reach me at here is 1-800-1-Scamco.

TIM: Well that's easy, I think I can remember that.

JOHN: Even without that powder, huh? Ha, ha, ha. Now you're going to make your check out in the amount of $362 even.

TIM: And make that out to Scamco. Now that's for the vitamins, is that right?

JOHN: Yes, now we can do this one of two ways. I can either get the vacation certificate to you in the mail or I can walk down to shipping and have one of the boys put it into the vitamin box and we'll have the box and the vacation certificate on its way to you tomorrow, you'll receive it next week.

TIM: Why don't you do that.

JOHN: OK. Are you going to be home between say 1:00 and 4:00 tomorrow?

TIM: Yes.

JOHN: OK great. I'm going to have an overnight express delivery runner stop out there to pick up that check and I'll give you my account number so you won't have to pay for that. And then what's going to happen is they're going to confirm the pick-up on the phone and the box will be shipped off tomorrow so you'll probably be receiving that box within two or three days.

TIM: OK that sounds good.

JOHN: Great. Oh, let me give you that number: Scamco 1234. Do you have any questions?

TIM: No I don't think so.

JOHN: Well listen, you have yourself a really good week there and actually I'd suggest to ya, you know it's a little bit cold in Vegas in March? I would suggest the perfect time to go to Vegas is May.

TIM: Really?

JOHN: Oh it's beautiful. The desert is blooming—you know cactus have flowers—the lake's warm by then—the temperature is in the high 80s, it's great. And if you go there in August, its 120 degrees on that lake.

TIM: I better not wait that long then. Thanks for calling.

JOHN: You're welcome and you have yourself a good week.

TIM: Thank you.

By convincing Tim that Scamco is a legitimate company and that he is getting a fabulous free vacation and a great deal on vitamins, John is able to make the sale. This approach is the core of the vast majority of telemarketing pitches used today in the United States: free prize, 50 percent discount on merchandise, avoid gift tax, prompt delivery. And all over the telephone.

The key phrase that should always trigger your "alert" button when the phone rings is, "Congratulations, you've won." It is impossible to overemphasize this. If you hear these words, the only thing to do is HANG UP!

THE "ONE OF FOUR" PITCH

The "one of four" pitch is probably one of the oldest and most successful pitches used by telemarketing fraud operators today in the United States. It preys on the sweepstakes mentality much like the Las Vegas vacation certificate pitch. The only difference is that the "prizes" are better and, as you will see in part two of this pitch, the telemarketer uses the first prize as a pitch for the second one.

John is going to convince Bill that he has won a fabulous prize, although he won't say exactly which prize he has won. Then he will tell Bill that the promotion is being sponsored by the Rip-Off Water Filter Company and that in exchange for receiving the valuable prize, he is going to have to incur the minimal expense of buying a water filter.

As you read through this pitch, look for ways that John establishes the credibility of his company (the cloak of legitimacy) in order to assure Bill that the promotion is legitimate. Notice for example how he drops the names of established firms like Tiffany's of London, Cadillac, and Citibank and implies that his firm has a close working relationship with these companies. Try to put yourself in Bill's shoes and see if you would be convinced.

BILL: Hello?

JOHN: Hello, Bill? This is John Daniels. I'm with Scamco Redemption Center? I wanted to give you a call and let you know that you are a finalist in our grand prize sweepstakes. You will be guaranteed one of four fabulous prizes.

BILL: Is that right?

JOHN: That's right. Now the first prize is the big one. It's the 1993 Cadillac Seville. It is absolutely gorgeous.

BILL: You mean I've won that?

JOHN: Either that or $10,000 in cash, OK? Third prize is a one-half-carat diamond necklace from Tiffany's jewelers. It's got the half-carat in the middle and diamonds around it? And that's on an eighteen-carat twenty-four-inch gold chain. The retail value on that is $1,894. The fourth prize is a $1,000 shopping spree at the grocery store of your choice. Now those are the four prizes and you will be guaranteed one of them. What do you think of those prizes Bill??

BILL: That sounds great, but you know, I can't remember even entering a contest?

JOHN: I don't know. I wish I could enter this.

BILL: Believe me I'm not complaining.

JOHN: Ha, ha, ha. What we do Bill is we contact the various prize winners that the companies want involved in these promotions. As you well know, promotions of this type are a write-off for the company.

BILL: Uh-huh.

JOHN: Now Bill, I know you weren't born yesterday, so you're probably wondering who you have to shoot, right?

BILL: Well I wasn't going to say anything but, what's the catch?

JOHN: Yeah, well no matter what, you are guaranteed one of those four prizes. You are guaranteed either a 1993 Cadillac Seville, $10,000 in cash, the diamond necklace from Tiffany's, or the $1,000 shopping spree at a grocery store. Now that has been mailed to you in writing by the way. You might have seen the envelope, it was a large yellow envelope and it had a red zip mail on the front of it? OK, good. Just to let you know. Nowadays you gotta be careful right?

BILL: That's true.

JOHN: You betcha. Now, for the companies who sponsor this, they need to have invoices for the write-off. OK? So we are asking you to try out a brand new line of water filters. Do you have a water filter at your house now, because we do have other sponsors?

BILL: I don't think so. But what would I need with a water filter?

JOHN: Well as you well know, in the United States, it has been discovered that there are literally tens of thousands of dump areas. And what has happened is toxic chemicals have gotten into the ground waters.

BILL: Yeah, but that's not true in Seattle. I live in Seattle, it's beautiful here, the Northwest, we have lots of rain, clear water, clear air. That can't possibly be true in Seattle.

JOHN: That's great, but you never know. There's natural water sources like, have you ever been to the Sierra mountains?

BILL: Yes.

JOHN: You know how you can't drink the water there? Out of the stream?

BILL: I didn't know that.

JOHN: Yeah, because you get sick. Because there's micro-organisms in there, OK? The bottom line is that you'll get better drinking water, better for your body, better for your family, no matter where you live.

BILL: I will admit that my drinking water doesn't taste that great but I always thought that was just cause the city screwed it up—you know, let the government get involved with something and they'll screw it up every time.

JOHN: Exactly, Exactly—ha, ha, ha. Now this isn't ours by the way. This is the Rip-Off water filter. The Rip-Off water filter—you can hook it up and it'll take care of your whole house. Alright? It says here that the wash ends up better, you even take cleaner showers, the whole nine yards.

BILL: Now this isn't something I have to buy is it, because I thought you said I won something?

JOHN: Oh you have won. Obviously the sponsors need an invoice for the write-off.

BILL: What does that mean?

JOHN: Basically, that means that to give you a prize? To be able to guarantee a certain amount of people get in on the prize—there's only one thousand people who are guaranteed in on these prizes, OK? Now there is only one first prize. There is only one Cadillac Seville. So your chances are one out of a thousand. However, the $10,000 in cash? They are giving that out to fifty people.

BILL: Wow, fifty people out of a hundred?

JOHN: No out of a thousand. Then they are splitting the necklace and the thousand-dollar shopping spree. Now obviously there is a lot that goes into this. Included in with the water filter, we have information on Cadillac, we have information on Tiffany's, we have information on Citibank, and we have information on the National Association of Grocers because they sponsor these prizes. What happens is by federal law, at random, the names are selected from the central database and that is overseen by Price-Waterhouse. I'm sure you've heard of them before.

BILL: Yes, I have.

JOHN: So that's how it works. And obviously, Rip-Off water filter wants an invoice, so they are going to be sending you a water filter, this is a household model—V6247—it will last for a full year without having to replace any of the filters inside and then after that . . . Obviously Bill, if you like it for a year, you're going to buy the water filter from them every year, too. This is just another way these big companies do marketing—it just so happens that you got lucky and the computer picked your name.

BILL: So in other words, I get this water filter but they're banking on the fact that I'll buy new filters from them every year?

JOHN: Oh, of course.

BILL: I see, there's no free lunch.

JOHN: No it's not a free lunch but I gotta tell ya Bill, this one's pretty cheap. As a matter of fact, I'm trying to work it out so I can get one of those water filters for my house. I mean I think my water's OK or whatever, but you never know number one and I have small kids and this takes the lead out of the water, OK?

BILL: Oh really? I have an eight-year-old grandson myself.

JOHN: Now what they are going to do is release this to you at wholesale price. Normally it retails for . . . its comparison is the Culligan by the way . . . normally this retails at $942 and they're going to let you have it wholesale at $364. And they're going to let you go ahead and put that on Visa, Mastercard, or American Express. That way you get to see the filter before you even get the bill.

BILL: I see. When do I get my prize? When do I know if I've won the car or not? How does all of that work?

JOHN: OK that's a real good question. What will happen, and this is also by federal law, you know the government, is—

BILL: You can't even go to the bathroom anymore without checking with the federal government first.

JOHN: It makes you wonder—like I wonder here sometimes why do the owners actually put up with it? I mean, they're just faced with so many things they have to pay for, it's just ridiculous. But thank God a lot of it's write-offs. And if they take away write-offs, it's going to hurt all of us.

BILL: And that's what they're talking about here, huh? A write-off?

JOHN: Oh yeah, and I'll tell you what. These corporations want to get these write-offs in before the new Congress and the new President start eliminating some of these write-offs.

BILL: I hear ya there.

JOHN: You know, you read it in *Time, Newsweek,* the whole nine yards. So you are guaranteed one of those four prizes I mentioned.

Now the way it's going to work is within the next month and by the way, we don't know what you've won yet because they won't tell us until a week before a federal regulator is available. We have to pay his airfare here. We have to put him up at the Hilton he wants to stay at OK? We have to give him a rental car. And this is someone working for us! The government!

BILL: I'll be darned.

JOHN: So that's how it works. It has to be overseen and then what they do is we even had to hire a bonded computer operator. And what's going to happen is the federal regulator will be there when the computer operator hits a certain random selection program and that's how the people are going to be selected for the prizes.

BILL: I see.

JOHN: You will be notified in the mail once again. You've already got that notification that you are one of the four. Then you'll go from there. It's that simple.

BILL: So what do I have to do?

JOHN: Quite simply, what I would suggest right now is—uh—let me ask you, did you want to put this on Visa, Mastercard, American Express, Discover?

BILL: I guess I could give you my Visa—or is it going to be shipped to me? Maybe I could just pay for it after I receive it.

JOHN: Well that's what you are going to be doing with the credit card. See, the credit card companies protect you. As a matter of fact, if you put this on Visa, Visa guarantees that if you see another water filter the same model, same brand whatever—cheaper anywhere in the next year? You get double the difference.

BILL: I didn't realize Visa did that for me—I just thought they charged me a lot of interest.

JOHN: Visa does a lot of things, they really do. If you get the $10,000 in cash, you got it from them because they're sponsoring this. So I'd suggest you go ahead and put it on your Visa number—what is that?

BILL: Well hold on a minute, I'm going to have to get that—can you hold on a minute?

JOHN: Yeah.

BILL: My grandson was playing with my wallet again. Ready?

JOHN: Yep.

BILL: That's 4248 0803 9319 0029.

JOHN: OK and when does that expire?

BILL: That's 10/94.

JOHN: OK and is that under your name?

BILL: Yes.

JOHN: Let me read that number back to you to make sure they've got the right number here—and by the way, we don't keep this in any of our records—this is going to go off to Rip-Off water filters so that's how it will show up on your bill. Let me read that back to you—that's 4248 0803 9319 0029. Is that right?

BILL: That's right.

JOHN: Expiration 10/94?

BILL: You got it.

JOHN: OK I tell you what, grab a pen.

BILL: OK.

JOHN: My name once again is John Daniels. And my number is 1-800-1-Scamco.

BILL: OK.

JOHN: Go ahead and do this. You seem like a pretty good guy there. Give me a call in a couple of weeks after you've got the water filter out there and I'll be able to tell you if they've had the drawing yet and, you know, tell you what's going on there.

BILL: Kind of give me a jump on things?

JOHN: Sure why not.

BILL: So how much is that water filter again?

JOHN: That water filter is $364.

BILL: But I'm getting a good deal on it. Is that right?

JOHN: You're getting it wholesale. I don't know, is wholesale a good deal? Yeah, I would hook that water filter up right away especially because you've got an eight-year-old running around there and they say that lead can come into the ground at different times. Some yards that are on old streets often have real high levels of lead.

BILL: Well I live in a house that's seventy years old, should I be worried about that?

JOHN: Definitely. If I were you, I would call the city or county water department and tell them you want a testing kit for the lead content in your yard. Then they'll send it to you for free or for five dollars and you can test for lead content. Anyway, look for that in the mail and I'll talk to you in a couple of weeks.

BILL: OK. Good-bye.

This pitch shows the pure salesmanship skills that someone like John T. has at his disposal. Did you notice how hard he works to establish the firm's credibility?

"What happens is by federal law, at random, the names are selected from the central data base and that is overseen by Price-Waterhouse. I'm sure you've heard of them before."

Add to that the part about the federal regulators regularly visiting their operation to ensure that no hanky-panky is going on and you have a solid sales pitch for the firm's credibility. Another part of the pitch is to assure the victim that he can get his money back at any time:

"As a matter of fact, if you put this on Visa, Visa guarantees that if you see another water filter the same model, same brand whatever—cheaper anywhere in the next year, you get double the difference."

Finally, John gives Bill the "50 percent off" close, only he represents the discount on the water filter to be more like 66 percent ($942 retail, $364 wholesale). I asked John what the company normally paid for these water filters.

"It would depend on how many we bought at one time of course. But I recall the average cost to us was about $80," John said. "This means we were marking things up by about 400 percent and telling people they were getting a huge discount. It worked like a charm."

THE "ONE OF FOUR" PITCH—PART TWO

In this transcript, about two weeks later, John actually gets a call back from Bill inquiring about his participation in the promotion. With masterful skill, John guides Bill to the box that was just delivered to his home that day and tells him to open it. He finds a diamond necklace from Tiffany's and is elated. This gives John a foot in the door to "reload" Bill on a second promotion involving "even better" prizes and the purchase of makeup.

His goal here is to get another $374 out of Bill. Read carefully or you'll miss just how clever he is at his craft.

JOHN: Hello, Scamco Redemption Center. This is John Daniels. Can I help you?

BILL: Yes. This is Bill Erickson calling. I talked to you a couple of weeks ago about a prize I won and I was just calling to see if you knew anything about the drawing yet?

JOHN: Bill, how are you doing? I'm glad you called. Hang on a second, cause I think they had that drawing—let me look here. I tell you what? You didn't get the box yet did ya?

BILL: You mean the water filter box? I just got it today and I haven't opened it yet.

JOHN: Go open the box and then come back to the phone.

BILL: OK, I'll be right back. (Gets box.) I've got it right here.

JOHN: Open it up and on the top in between some white foam padding, there is going to be something. I want you to take that out.

BILL: What is this?

JOHN: See the little bag lying on top there—open it up.

BILL: What the. . .

JOHN: Bill, congratulations! You won the diamond necklace—it's in your hand!

BILL: Is that what this is—I tell ya, the wife is going to love this. Is this a real diamond?

JOHN: Look at it. What does it say on the top? Tiffany's jewelers.

BILL: Gee.

JOHN: That's going to get you more than a hug and a kiss tonight, huh?

BILL: My wife really will like this. But I thought I was going to have to call you to see if I had won. I didn't know they were going to send it to me.

JOHN: It says right here on the computer screen. Cause you know, we handle hundreds of these drawings and things, it says on the computer screen that um I guess the federal regulator came in three days after you and I spoke. They chose the prizes and what they did was they sent the prizes and the water filters together so they could mark that as a sales premium for their tax write-off. So congratulations!

BILL: So what is this baby worth?

JOHN: Look at the certificate of authenticity from the London Precious Jewel Gallery.

BILL: I see that. $1,847. Wow.

JOHN: Now we do need for you to send a picture of your wife wearing the necklace.

BILL: Why do I have to do that?

JOHN: Take her out on the town. Be romantic Bill. Now whoever is in the picture needs to sign the "model's release form." You'll see the model's release form, it's folded up—it's right behind the certificate of authenticity.

BILL: Oh yeah, here it is, here it is.

JOHN: Good, cause we're using the pictures in a few new catalogs. Anyway, you did real well this time, so congratulations again Bill.

BILL: Thank you. I'm still not exactly sure how this happened.

JOHN: Have you ever seen the people on TV like with the clearinghouse sweepstakes and they won the prizes on "Let's Make a Deal" and stuff like that?

BILL: Yeah.

JOHN: Well, that's the same difference. OK? You're just getting lucky. Now Bill while I've got you on the line, I need to explain to you that they have decided to go ahead—they think that the Congress is going to act pretty quickly on the write-off? So they've decided to go ahead and extend the drawing here.

So what they're going to do is take all of the prize winners from the first phase of the promotion—enter you into the next phase of the promotion—this way everyone gets something nice and our repeat customers end up with the top prizes.

You and I both know that if you wind up with a big cash prize, you're going to be doing business with the sponsors for a long time to come, am I right?

BILL: That is more than likely.

JOHN: This time around, they've ended up with a few more dollars than expected. So rather than sending it off to the White House—ha, ha, ha—they're going to upgrade the prizes.

BILL: You mean I could win another prize?

JOHN: Oh, they're better than ever. Get a pen and a piece of paper— I'll hang on.

BILL: Got it.

JOHN: The first prize is another 1993 Cadillac Seville. Only this time, they are giving away three of them. Second prize is the $10,000 in cash again. This time, they are giving it out to 150 people. Third is a lake boat—perfect for fishing or water skiing—retail value on that is $4,000. And fourth is a $2,000 shopping spree at any store of your choice that takes Visa or Mastercard. You're guaranteed one of those four prizes.
Now let me see here—Rip-Off water filters feels like you've got enough to meet your needs there—so what they've done is transferred contest credits over to—let me see—Phyllis Diller makeup. You're married right?

BILL: Right.

JOHN: OK good. Bill, the beauty of this is that you don't have to take a big distributor-sized box. You can thank our accountants for that. We've arranged to take a distributor-sized box of makeup—you know, everyone's wife or girlfriend wears makeup—this is that same makeup that's on TV—those infomercials that have Cher and all of the rest of them on there.

BILL: Oh I have seen those.

JOHN: This is a two-year supply of makeup, guaranteed. Gee, it has a list of everything. Now the distributor-sized box is only $374. That's broken down to one-quarter of an order, OK, oh this is nice. You know what they're doing with the other three-quarters of an order?

BILL: What's that?

JOHN: They're donating them to an abused women's shelter.

BILL: Oh really. That is nice.

JOHN: Well, you know, if you look good you feel good. That's nice. Actually, in the real world Bill? That allows them to right it off for retail. It also helps a few people. OK, you're going to receive everything here in about two weeks and what we're going to go ahead and do—you know they still don't know when that regulator is going to be back for this one. Do you still have my number?

BILL: I think so.

JOHN: OK good. And then what we're going to go ahead and do on this makeup, so that you have that same protection is we're just going to go ahead and put it on that Visa card again.

BILL: I guess I don't understand. How come I am entered into another contest?

JOHN: Same as last time, OK? What happens—last time, you would have won the necklace no matter what, OK? Cause you won one of those four prizes. But since you were smart enough to go ahead and say yeah, I'll go ahead and take one of the sponsor's water filters, which is a real good filter, and you got a great price on it—because you were smart enough to do that, then they bumped all those people up to this one.

As a matter of fact, let me see here—yeah, there's actually only 920 people, 80 people decided not to take the filter, so those 80 people missed out of this four. So you're guaranteed either a 1993 Cadillac Seville, $10,000 in cash, the lake boat, or the $2,000 shopping spree. Ya can't beat that with a stick Bill.

BILL: That really sounds pretty good.

JOHN: OK, great Bill, any questions, you've got my number. And I don't think they're going to have, you know, another one after this one, but we're also going to send you out a list of some of our sponsors and we'd really appreciate it if you could do business with them whenever you can. You have yourself a good week.

BILL: I will thank you.

As you read this script, did you notice how John got Bill to bond with him?

JOHN: Now we do need for you to send a picture of your wife wearing the necklace.

BILL: Why do I have to do that?

JOHN: Take her out on the town. Be romantic Bill.

John also cleverly transitioned Bill from one promotion to the next:

JOHN: You're just getting lucky. Now Bill, while I've got you on the line, I need to explain to you that they have decided to go ahead . . . and extend the drawing here. So what they're going to do is take all of the prize winners from the first phrase of the promotion—enter you into the next phase of the promotion—this way everyone gets something nice and our repeat customers end up with top prizes.

I hope that one of the conclusions you will draw from reading these pitches is that these salesmen are good—very good—and that it is dangerous to spend any time talking to them because they can be so convincing. Also, notice the various ploys John used on Bill. The "one of four" pitch has all five of the elements of fraud which have been discussed throughout this book:

- ✆ The "cloak of legitimacy" is used throughout the pitch when John refers to the "federal regulator" and how the owners of the company are burdened with the IRS as are all "legitimate" companies.

- ✆ The "sweepstakes mentality" is the foundation of the pitch: winning a valuable prize in exchange for purchasing a relatively inexpensive water filter.

- ⓒ The "charm factor" is used when John relates to Bill about how screwed up the government is. He also attempts to befriend Bill by relating to Bill's relationship with his wife.

- ⓒ The "news as a hook" theme is touched upon when John discusses the reason for the second promotion: the new administration might eliminate tax write-offs.

- ⓒ Finally, the "follower mentality" is present to some extent. John talks about how he has a water filter in his home because he has small children and he is concerned for their health and safety. He then suggests Bill should have a similar concern for his eight-year-old grandson.

"I was so convincing, that I started to believe my own pitches," said John. "It is amazing what can happen when a strong personality like me gets his sights on something—or someone," he said.

THE SILVER INVESTMENT PITCH

In this pitch, John has been talking to Rosie over a period of several weeks about managing her investment portfolio. He called her initially after she had filled out a lead card expressing her interest in getting more information about gold and silver investments. Rosie is a widow whose husband passed away two years ago.

This pitch is the culmination of very careful groundwork John laid during his previous conversations with Rosie. Hours and hours were spent each week talking to her about everything and anything he could think of to endear himself to her. The main strategy is to talk about personal things, in this case, Rosie's work at the senior center, her family, and especially those grandkids.

"The set up calls for these investors are really more important to selling them than the close. I became a confidant, a psychotherapist, a friend—anything but someone trying to sell investments. It was pretty easy to endear myself to these lonely people—and believe me—I'm not proud of it," said John.

One of the telephone fraud operators who stole over $20,000 from Emma, the woman profiled in chapter 1, echoed just how ruthless some of these frauders can be. When I called his office in Las Vegas, I asked him to consider how he would feel if someone had taken $20,000 from his mother. He said she was simply "buying companionship."

"Isn't that an awful large some of money for a little companionship?" I asked.

"Heck, I know people in this town who would pay $5 million for a friend. No, I don't think $20,000 is too much to pay," replied the phone operator.

What you are about to read is the "close" part of a series of phone calls that took place over a period of months. John's goal is to convince Rosie that he is going to take care of all of her financial investment needs. And why shouldn't she believe him? He has become one of the only human beings on earth who calls her to ask how her day went.

JOHN: Hello, Rosie? How are you doing?

ROSIE: Hi. Is this John?

JOHN: Yes it is. How was your day today?

ROSIE: Oh, busy.

JOHN: Oh? What did you do?

ROSIE: The usual, I had several errands to run and then I had to go to lunch at the senior center.

JOHN: And how was the senior center?

ROSIE: The same as always, I've been volunteering down there for about ten years now. It's nice because I see all my friends.

JOHN: How is Fred's leg doing?

ROSIE: Much better, much better—he complains about it an awful lot, but I think it's doing better.

JOHN: You know it's a good thing that those people have you there Rosie.

ROSIE: Well, thank you.

JOHN: It really is. God bless you. I think what you're doing is just great.

ROSIE: It's nice of you to say that.

JOHN: I wanted to call you to give you the good news.

ROSIE: What's that?

JOHN: Silver went up.

ROSIE: It did?

JOHN: Yes it did. I told you it would go up didn't I? Now it's taken a little longer than we thought it would but what the heck, with this election and everything, anything can happen.

ROSIE: That's true. What do you think I should do?

JOHN: Rosie, basically what I have been doing is analyzing your portfolio. Let me see. How much did you say you had in real estate?

ROSIE: Oh I don't know. I don't know what anything is worth any more.

JOHN: Just basically, the last time your accountant took a look.

ROSIE: There are those two rental properties, I'd say they are worth about $100,000 each. Then there's the condo I'm living in now, I'd say it's all worth about $300,000.

JOHN: You know that market has bottomed out too?

ROSIE: The real estate market? You know, Harold always told me that real estate will never go down. It will always go up and that is why I have held on to those rentals.

JOHN: And Harold was right. Harold was 100 percent right. Now I am going to be really blunt with you. If this were thirty years ago, I'd say yes you have the time to wait on the real estate. But what has happened here is your portfolio is unbalanced. Things are not the same as they were forty years ago.

ROSIE: What do you mean by unbalanced?

JOHN: Quite simply, you want to keep a certain percentage of your investments in short-term investments, mid-range investments, and long-range investments, am I right?

ROSIE: I do remember Harold saying something like that. I am so new to this. This is still quite new to me. It's only been two years since Harold passed on and I'm still having trouble with this.

JOHN: That's why I'm here Rosie. I am going to take care of you. I'm going to take care of you the same way I take care of my mom. I'm going to take care of you the same way I take care of my grandmother.

ROSIE: That's nice.

JOHN: That is just the way it should be. I was raised in a generation where we were taught to respect our elders. I don't know what's happening nowadays. My goodness. You watch the news and these kids are shooting people. It's ridiculous, but that's not the generation I'm from.

ROSIE: It's frightening.

JOHN: It really is. It pays for you to be secure Rosie, it really, really does. Hang on a second I got another call I'll be right back. . . .

ROSIE: OK.

JOHN: (after several seconds) Rosie.

ROSIE: Yes.

JOHN: That was one of the board members. I told him I'd call him back. I tell you, I've been working so hard lately. They tell me I should do it while I can, are they right?

ROSIE: I guess so.

JOHN: Ha, ha, ha. Now Rosie, let me see here. You're seventy-two years young now, am I right?

ROSIE: Ha, ha. Yes.

JOHN: Now I am always going to be straightforward with you. And I don't think you'd want it any other way would you?

ROSIE: Why no.

JOHN: OK. Rosie, right now at your time in life, you need to plan your portfolio so that you have short-term and mid-range investments. Now I'm not saying get rid of all the property, that would be crazy. What I am suggesting—let's see—you're living in the condo, right?

ROSIE: Yes.

JOHN: So do you get a positive cash flow on both rental properties?

ROSIE: I live off of part of that rental income.

JOHN: How much income do you get total?

ROSIE: I get $300 a month from each property.

JOHN: Rosie, go get your calculator and a pencil, I'll hang on.

ROSIE: OK.

JOHN: Now Rosie, you're getting $300 a month positive cash flow from each property. Now which property would you say needs the most improvements?

ROSIE: Probably the one down on Burton Avenue.

JOHN: I want you to do this. I want you to multiply $300 times 12.

ROSIE: OK.

JOHN: And what do you get?

ROSIE: $3,600.

JOHN: OK. Now I want you to multiply that times ten years.

ROSIE: $3,600 times ten years? That would be $36,000.

JOHN: OK. Now, what did you say that property on Burton is worth?

ROSIE: How much is it valued at? Probably about 150.

JOHN: 150. OK. And you've just about got that paid off? Didn't Harold's life insurance pay that off?

ROSIE: It's almost paid off. I think there is another year to go on it.

JOHN: And how much do you think that last year will cost you, about $400?

ROSIE: I think I had about a 4 percent mortgage on that.

JOHN: Oh my God, you're kidding me. When did you get the mortgage?

ROSIE: That was in 1964. That was back when you could afford to buy property, you know?

JOHN: I know, my wife and I, even though I make a great income, my wife and I both work because I have eleven properties myself. But I'll tell ya, I took a little bit of a hit when these properties went down in value. So what I'm going to do—these properties are going to go down for another year or two, I don't care what anyone says. As a matter of fact, I've been starting to sell some of mine here. Now what I want you to do—I want you to put down on that piece of paper $150,000.

ROSIE: OK.

JOHN: Let's say that over the next ten years, you need to put a new roof on that Burton Avenue property. How much would that cost—maybe $3,000?

ROSIE: Gee, I really have no idea.

JOHN: And let's say the furnace breaks down and needs to be replaced at a cost of $3,000. Now instead of getting $36,000 over the next ten years in rental income, you only get $30,000. Now right down $30,000 right next to the $150,000. Now I want you to subtract $30,000 from $150,000.

ROSIE: OK. That's $120,000.

JOHN: That's $120,000 Rosie that could be working for you for the next ten years. The way you've got it set up now, it's like your money is in a CD. And a CD is a great place to park your money until a real investment comes around. Now I'm going to tell you something Rosie, every time you see major wars, you see silver go up. Did you catch the big gold and silver run back in 1980?

ROSIE: Why, no I didn't.

JOHN: Well I did. And so did a lot of my clients. And I'll tell you what Rosie—EVERY ONE OF THEM—every single one of those clients, with the exception of two—are wealthy now. And do you know why those two aren't wealthy?

ROSIE: Why?

JOHN: Because they got greedy. And I watched it happen. I had my girls call and tell those people to sell out because it was going to start to go down. And they got greedy and they didn't sell out. Which reminds me Rosie, when the silver hits 9, that's when we're going to want to sell.

ROSIE: How much is it now?

JOHN: Right now it's at $7.50. So it went up four cents. Now you gotta understand what's going on over there in Yugoslavia—the war? It's going to affect everything. Remember that Euro dollar they were going to start over in Europe? They have actually postponed on that. So silver is going to be going up. And did you know that during war time, they use more silver?

ROSIE: I didn't know that.

JOHN: Oh yeah. What do you think they build high-tech weaponry out of? What do you think is in photographs? Remember I told you every photograph that gets printed? Silver. Why do you think Kodak would spend $120 million on a silver recovery system for their processors? Why would they spend that much money?

ROSIE: Because it's worth it to them I guess.

JOHN: Exactly. Exactly. Now what I suggest we do here. Right now, you've only got $20,000 in silver. So, as far as short-term investments, your mid-range investments are taken care of with your mutual funds—don't touch the funds—they've dropped a little bit, but they're safe, you know what I'm saying? Now this is what you need to do. I strongly suggest you just go ahead and sell the house.

ROSIE: Sell the rental property? But I've had it for almost thirty years.

JOHN: That's great. And how much did you pay for it?

ROSIE: Well I'd have to get the old records out, but it definitely has gone up in value. That's one reason I'm hesitant to sell it—I think it will still go up. I think we paid $20,000 for it. Now it's worth $150,000. Shouldn't I just continue to hold on to it?

JOHN: Rosie, had you sold it two years ago, when it was worth about $180,000 or $190,000, you'd be sitting on an extra $30,000 or $40,000 today. I wish we were speaking at that time. Because I'll tell ya, if we were speaking at that time, I would have had you sell some of your properties. I sold everything I had at that time and then I started buying again about a year ago. It was a little bit soon, but I've gotten good deals on everything I've purchased, so I always make money. Some of us, we just have the Midas touch. Hang on a second, I've got another call. . . .

ROSIE: OK.

JOHN: (after a few seconds) Rosie? Yeah, I'm back now. Rosie, you sound a little bit hesitant and I can understand why you feel that way. I understand that making these financial decisions is new to you. And I understand that it is difficult. But I also understand Rosie that the only way I can show you how to become financially independent is by you following my lead.

Rosie, right now we are walking on a path out in the mountains. And we're walking along this path and there is a fork in the road. And you say, "John, I wanna go right" and I say, "Rosie why do you want to go right?" and you say, "because I've always gone right when the fork came in the road."

And I'm telling you Rosie that I've seen where that fork in the road goes—and we need to go left. And you need to have faith. You need to have faith in me, because I told you that I'm going to take care of you like I take care of my mother, I'm going to take care of you like I take care of my grandmother. And I'll tell you what Rosie, I'm going to take you down that right path. But you have to listen. And if there is anything you don't understand, for gosh sakes, ask me. Because I know.

ROSIE: What happens if I don't know how to sell property? I've never sold a house before. You're saying I should sell my house so I can invest in silver?

JOHN: Partially. Partially. I'm going to have you put some of that money into a stock, it's called Medco containment. It's a real safe stock. I'm going to have you put $10,000 in that. I figure that will bring you back anywhere from $40,000 to $60,000 within three to four years. The way I'm going to set you up Rosie is you're going to be able to live the life you've always wanted to live. You're going to be able to live out your golden years without one worry. And it's because you've got me in your corner. And I'm going to stay in your corner and I'm going to fight for you Rosie, because that's the kind of guy I am.

ROSIE: Well that's awfully nice of you. It's nice to have an honest-sounding man who can help me with these difficult decisions.

JOHN: Rosie, I'll even show you how to reconcile your checkbook, have you tried that yet?

ROSIE: Oh, now, I can do that, that's the one thing I'm sure of.

JOHN: You know how I do mine? My computer does it. It's great.

ROSIE: I don't understand those computers.

JOHN: Well, you don't have to. You've worked hard all your life. It's about time you started enjoying life and doing things you want to do.

ROSIE: Well, how do I get started. Should I contact a real estate agent or what?

JOHN: It's no problem. What I can do is have one of my girls contact an agent in you area. I have my computer network here and my computer tells me if an agent's good or not.

ROSIE: I see, so you can check out the agent for me.

JOHN: Rosie, I'm your lifeline to the financial marketplace. It's phenomenal. I have a program set up here that automatically tracks 1,200 different stocks under the parameters I have entered. I have a similar program for real estate. By tomorrow, I'll be able to tell you exactly what that house is worth. Now what's the address on that house?

ROSIE: I just knew you were going to ask me that. Just a minute now. That's 4012 Burton Avenue, Summitville, North Carolina 00124.

JOHN: Got it. OK Rosie, what I'm going to go ahead and do is I'm going to arrange for the Realtor to contact you. Now I'm going to be with you the whole way. This is as easy as walking a mile. And I'm going to walk that mile with you.

ROSIE: OK. Whatever you say John.

JOHN: Rosie, let me ask you, what's one thing that you always wanted to do that you never got around to doing? Like take a vacation or anything.

ROSIE: Well, I've never been to Paris before to see the Eiffel Tower.

JOHN: You always wanted to go?

ROSIE: Uh-huh. That's something I've always wanted to do but I never felt like I could afford it. The reason I don't like to spend my money is because I'd like to think I could leave something for my children and my grandchildren.

JOHN: You're going to.

ROSIE: Well, I want to make sure of that. Which is why I don't want to be real lavish on myself and go on wild trips to Europe and everything.

JOHN: Oh come on. You know what we can do? How many grandchildren do you have?

ROSIE: Five.

JOHN: You know what we can do that a lot of my clients have done?

ROSIE: What?

JOHN: We can get a few thousand dollars of silver for each of the grandkids.

ROSIE: Really?

JOHN: Then when it goes up? I'll tell ya Rosie, in twelve to fourteen months? Its going to triple or quadruple.

ROSIE: Really? That much.

JOHN: Oh yeah. You see, this way the kids get to see what it's like to live in America. The kids get to experience making their own investments—with gramma's help but . . . ha, ha, ha.

ROSIE: So they can follow it as it goes up.

JOHN: Right.

ROSIE: That does sound like a good idea. I am definitely interested in that.

JOHN: It can be a family affair. And you know what? You're going to Paris. How old are the grandkids?

ROSIE: They range in age from three to ten years old.

JOHN: Three to ten, alright. Do you have any friends who might want to go to Paris with you?

ROSIE: My sister. My sister and I have never really been on a big trip together and I think it would be fun.

JOHN: That is great. What's your sister's name?

ROSIE: Isabelle.

JOHN: Isabelle. Alrighty. When is Isabelle's birthday?

ROSIE: In October.

JOHN: And when is your birthday?

ROSIE: My birthday is in July.

JOHN: You know what? You gotta give yourself a birthday present. I was in Paris a few years ago. Unfortunately, we went in January for our convention. And is it cold—I was in Paris in the snow.

ROSIE: Oh really.

JOHN: And I'm so used to seeing those movies of Paris in the spring and the summer that I couldn't believe it. I didn't even bring a coat.

ROSIE: Shame on you.

JOHN: My charge cards went up a lot those two weeks. But I'll tell ya, it's absolutely gorgeous and you'd be surprised how many people speak English. But you know, that makes it convenient.

ROSIE: Is that right?

JOHN: And I want a postcard.

ROSIE. OK. So you'll get started on the real estate thing?

JOHN: Oh yeah, no big deal. No big deal. I'll take care of all of that for ya. If you want, I can even handle the entire transaction. I can just have my girl send out a power of attorney letter—no big deal—and what I'm going to do is create for you a winning portfolio that's gonna take care of you the way you need to be taken care of. It's going to take care of the kids for when—Heaven forbid—you leave us. But you know what, you're a pretty healthy gal.

ROSIE: Yes, I feel pretty good now. I was kind of down there for awhile after Harold died, but I think I'm getting my second wind.

JOHN: Well, you know it takes time to get over things like that and as time goes on, you just add to your family. I mean heck, it's like I told you last month, you're now part of my family of investors and when I say family Rosie, I mean family.

ROSIE: Well that's awfully nice.

JOHN: Well, it's a fact. We're all in this together. We all have to help each other. One thing my clients do is—I found out about Medco containment from an attorney client of mine. Of course I did my research, and I found out he was right. That's how it works around here, we all help each other. Hang on a second, I got a call . . . .

ROSIE: OK.

JOHN: (after a few seconds) Rosie, alright so this is what we are going to do. I will have my computer find us the best real estate agent in that area. At that time, my girl is going to send you out a power of attorney letter. All you need to do is sign it and send it back to me and then I'll take care of everything. Once we've sold the house—now we're not going to give it away—we're going to get a good deal on this house.

ROSIE: I sure hope so. I've had that house for nearly thirty years. Son number one and son number two came along while we were in that house.

JOHN: I think that is fantastic.

ROSIE: Well, I trust you John.

JOHN: Well, you should. You should.

ROSIE: I hope nothing goes wrong.

JOHN: Rosie, no way. When I get done here, you're going to make more money on that house than you thought you would, we're going to take some of it, we're going to get you some more mutual funds but I want you to try a couple of funds besides the ones you have now—you know, diversify? I'm going to show you how in the coming years you can get some of those mutual funds for the kids and the grandkids. Remember I explained to you you've got that inheritance tax? So by transferring some of your assets now, you will have saved thousands of dollars. That's money you can give to the grandkids and it just grows and grows and will leave you a virtual living legacy.

ROSIE: That sounds wonderful.

JOHN: We'll then invest some in the silver, and then you're going to invest some in Medco containment and then we're going to have a little parking fund. I might have you get a six-month CD. CD's are a great place to park your money until a real investment comes around.

ROSIE: Thanks for taking all this time with me.

JOHN: That's no problem at all dear. I want you to know that I'm here for you all the time.
If you ever need me, you make sure you pick up the phone and you call me. You have a good night.

ROSIE: Thank you.

JOHN: God bless.

What a con! John is going to show Rosie a way that she can live the dreams she has had all of her life. She is going to make more money than she every dreamed possible and she is finally, after all these years, going to be able to take that trip to Paris.

If any of the things John said in this pitch were true, maybe those con artists who claim they are paid to provide companionship by talking to widows would have a point. But virtually nothing John said in this pitch was true. He made up the names of stocks, and convinced her to sell rental properties which were stable.

This pitch represents the bread and butter of the telemarketing fraud industry. John used it as early as 1977 and the attorney general offices in fifty states and the FBI are working on investigations involving this pitch as I write this.

Now that you have read through five of the most common approaches used to defraud older adults over the phone, it is time to have some fun with them. During the 1980s, I spent a considerable amount of time doing skits of various fraud schemes at senior centers. The reason for acting out the bank examiner hoax or pigeon drop (see chapter 3) was to graphically portray exactly how con artists practice their craft, much like what was done in this chapter. Sometimes I would arrange ahead of time to have a person from the senior center act out the skit with me in order to give it some local color.

The best way to learn these pitches inside and out so you will never fall for them is to act them out. Find a friend who you feel might be vulnerable to telemarketers and reenact one or more of these transcripts. Simply give your friend a copy of this book or just make a copy of the script, assign roles, and read the pitch aloud. If you really want to have fun, tape record your reenactment so you can play it back and hear yourselves!

If you do this exercise, two things will happen. First, at some point both you and your friend will bust up laughing. Second, you will fully digest the material so that when a real con artist calls, you will be truly ready for him. Who said fraud fighting isn't fun!

Hang Up on Phony Offers!

Keep this by your phone and answer the following questions
the next time you are called by a telephone solicitor.

ASK THE PHONE SOLICITOR:

1. Are you selling something?_____

2. Who am I talking to?   Business Name:_____

                                    Address:_____

                                    City/State:_____

                                    Telephone:_____

3. Is your business registered to telemarket in _____ (your state)? _____

4. What is your registration number?_____

5. Will you give me time to check with my local Better Business Bureau and the Attorney General's
Consumer Protection Unit?_____

ASK YOURSELF:

1. Do I need the product, prize, or service?_____

2. Do I have to make a purchase in order to get my "prize"? (*You shouldn't!*)_____

3. Do they want my credit card number, bank account number, or social security number? (*Never
give any personal numbers over the phone!*) _____

4. Can I afford to lose any money?_____

5. Does it sound too good to be true?_____

ASK THE ATTORNEY GENERAL'S CONSUMER PROTECTION UNIT:

1. What is the above company's telemarketing registration number?_____

2. Please send me information on the above company._____

CHAPTER

7

CALL TO ACTION: BECOME AN AMERICAN FRAUD FIGHTER

"Every violation of truth is not only a sort of suicide in the liar, but is a stab at the health of human society."

—Emerson

Now that you have read about virtually every kind of scam that is out there in the marketplace, it is time to take the final steps toward becoming an American fraud fighter.

The goal of this book is to empower every older adult in the country so he or she will not become a victim of fraud. In order to achieve this goal, we need your help. If you have thoroughly read the material up to this point, you are nearly a fraud fighter already and can help wage war against the swindlers who pervade this nation.

There are three final steps you need to take before hitting the battlefield. They are outlined in this chapter, and include the following: take the "empowered consumer" quiz; learn the general prevention strategies for preventing phone, door-to-door, mail, and infomercial fraud; and apply the intervention strategies to help others avoid fraud.

THE EMPOWERED CONSUMER QUIZ

First, in order to assess your level of empowerment, take the following quiz. Most people will have little trouble passing this quiz with flying colors. However, if you do have problems, consider going back and reviewing the material again before proceeding with this chapter.

1. When someone calls you and says, "Congratulations! You've just won one of four fabulous prizes!" your response is:

_____ A. Great! What do I have to do to get my fabulous prize?

_____ B. I won? But I don't remember entering a contest. I sure could use the $10,000 cash prize though . . . tell me more.

_____ C. I don't believe you. All of these prize promotions are scams—good-bye!

2. Someone knocks on your door and says, "Hi ma'am. I was doing a roofing job down the street and I noticed your roof needs work. I'll give you 50 percent off to fix your roof." Your response is:

_____ A. Oh my. There's something wrong with my roof? Yes, I better get it taken care of immediately. When can you start?

_____ B. If there is something wrong, I better fix it. But I don't trust just anyone. You'll have to give me a written statement of costs first.

_____ C. Sorry, but I don't do business with strangers who knock on my door. If my roof needs repairs, I will look up contractors in the yellow pages and get three written estimates.

3. You read an advertisement in the newspaper stating that you could lose up to 90 percent of your estate by having to go through expensive probate procedures. It suggests buying a living trust to avoid probate and the costs involved. You decide to:

_____ A. Set up an appointment with a living trust company—you figure if it really can save tens of thousands in probate costs, then it would be worth the $2,000 to $4,000 fee.

_____ B. Ask your own attorney whether a living trust would save your estate money since your attorney isn't selling living trusts and would give you objective advice.

_____ C. Go listen to a seminar on living trusts given by a living trust salesperson before you decide to buy.

4. You receive in the mail a sweepstakes entry form that asks you to solve a word puzzle and send between $5.00 and $30 in order to be eligible to win a $25,000 grand prize. You respond by:

_____ A. Solving the puzzle and sending in the $5.00, figuring it's a small amount of money and you may win $25,000.

_____ B. Throwing the mailer away since it is nothing more than junk mail and responding will likely get you on someone's mailing list.

_____ C. Solving the puzzle and sending in $30 in order to have a better chance of winning.

5. You receive a call from the American Association of Paralyzed Veterans asking for a charitable contribution. You respond as follows:

_____ A. You agree to send the caller a $25 contribution.

_____ B. You ask the caller to send you written information about the charity before you give, including their state registration number and the percentage of the contribution that goes to the charity versus the fund-raiser.

_____ C. You tell the caller you will give a donation if he or she tells you over the phone what percentage of the donation goes to the fund-raiser versus the charity.

6. A person calls you claiming to be from a large New York City brokerage house. He says he has a new mutual fund that is guaranteed to pay a 15 percent yield. He wants you to invest $10,000. You respond by:

_____ A. Telling the caller that you do not make investments over the telephone to people whom you do not know, and promptly hanging up.

_____ B. Telling the caller you want a prospectus and other written information to be sent to you in the mail and then you'll consider it.

_____ C. Agreeing to wire the caller $10,000 because you are currently only receiving a 5 percent return on that money. Sure it's risky, but it would represent a 300 percent increase in yield.

7. A man calls you claiming to be an FBI agent. He says he is investigating an employee at your bank who is embezzling money. He asks you to go and withdraw $2,000 from the bank so he can inspect the bills. You respond in the following manner:

_____ A. You agree to help, since it is the FBI, and you don't want a dishonest person working at your bank.

_____ B. You tell the caller he's crazy since you know that neither the police nor the FBI would ever ask a customer to participate in a bank investigation. You hang up on the caller.

_____ C. You are skeptical, so when the man gives you the number for the local FBI office so you can verify what he's saying, you agree to verify the story by calling the number and then getting back to him.

8. One week after your spouse dies, a man appears at your door claiming to be a Bible salesman. He shows you a gold-inlayed version of the King James Bible with your name engraved in it and suggests that your spouse ordered it for you. He asks for your spouse and says there is a bill for $85 owing. You respond by saying:

_____A. My spouse died last week, but if he/she wanted me to have it then of course I'll pay for it.

_____B. My spouse died last week but he/she would have never ordered such a thing without telling me about it. Go away. (You close the door in the man's face.)

_____C. My spouse is gone and it seems awfully odd that my spouse would have done this because he/she was not what you would call a "religious" person. But I guess I'll buy it anyway since it will be something to remember him/her by.

9. You receive a letter in the mail from an attorney's office in Texas. The letter says the firm specializes in locating lost assets for people and they have found some unclaimed property belonging to you. They say if you agree to give them 33 percent of the property's value, they will tell you where it is. You respond by:

_____A. Signing the form they enclosed and sending it back, figuring that getting two-thirds of something is better than getting nothing.

_____B. Ignoring the letter altogether, figuring it's just another scam.

_____C. Acknowledging the letter not by agreeing to the lawyer's terms, but by beginning your own independent search for the unclaimed property. You start contacting the departments of revenue in states where you may have had relatives or where you lived in the past to see if the unclaimed property rolls list abandoned property in your name.

10. You receive a card in the mail that says you have won either a new car, $10,000 in cash, a European vacation, or a diamond necklace. It instructs you to call a 900 number to find out what you have won. You respond by:

_____A. Throwing the mailer away since the 900 number will result in a charge on your phone bill.

_____B. Calling the number even though you realize there is a charge for the call, thinking it must be worth it if the worst prize is a diamond necklace.

_____C. Deciding to write the company that sent you the mailer to find out what you have won so that you won't have to pay the cost of the 900 call.

●●

Now that you have read everything there is to know about how fraud schemes work, you are officially qualified to become an American fraud fighter. Since many potential victims of fraud will not have read this book, it is important for you to identify these people and intervene on their behalf when appropriate.

Start with sharing this quiz with friends or relatives to find out how they do on it. If your friend gets less than eight or nine correct answers, you might consider loaning him or her this book. Another way to both identify and help potential fraud victims is to make copies of the Empowered Consumer Quiz and take them to senior centers to help older adults assess their vulnerability to fraud. You may be able to have the senior center make copies for you. If they ask what your credentials are for administering such a quiz, tell them you have completed the *Schemes and Scams* course on how to become an American fraud fighter and you want to share your knowledge with others who may be vulnerable to fraud.

GENERAL PREVENTION STRATEGIES

The three main ways that you will be approached are through phone calls, door-to-door scams, or the mail. Although the entire book has listed prevention strategies for various schemes, here are some more specific strategies for preventing victimization in each of these categories.

Telephone Fraud

Anyone who has read this book realizes that phone fraud is probably the biggest single way con artists defraud people. John made a handsome living for nearly ten years by swindling people over the phone and it has been estimated that of the 140,000 firms using telemarketing in the United States today, up to 10 percent of them are fraudulent operations. Given that many fraudulent rooms are making hundreds of thousands of calls each month, it is vital that you be prepared. There are five signs to look for anytime someone whom you do not know calls you on the phone:

***P**retends to be your friend*

***H**igh-pressure sales pitch*

***O**verly concerned about your personal life*

***N**o written agreement for your attorney and accountant*

***E**xpects you to pay money for your "free" prize*

Pretends to be your friend

If the caller sounds overly friendly and is saying things like, "I love the sound of your voice" or "Are you really seventy-five years young? I can't believe it," then watch out. He or she wants to be your friend just long enough to steal your money.

High-pressure sales pitch

If the caller is pressuring you by saying things like, "You have to buy today or you won't get the discount" or "In order to get your bonus gift, you must make a decision right now," then hang up the phone. There is no deal out there that has to be made right away—no deal worth doing that is.

Overly concerned about your personal life

If the caller is asking you lots of questions about the grandkids or what you do for fun during the day and he or she is a total stranger, hang up the phone. Con artists steal your money by becoming your friend first, then swindling you. Do not become friendly over the phone with a perfect stranger no matter how tempting it might be.

No written information available

If the caller is unwilling to send you written information about the offer, then do not do business with him—period. Any legitimate telemarketing company is going to be willing to write to you and explain the offer in more detail before you buy. This is also true for legitimate charitable solicitors.

Expects you to pay money in order to win a "free" prize

If the caller says you have won a prize, but you must buy something or pay a "gift tax" or some other kind of fee, hang up the phone. In most states, it is illegal for a caller to require payment in order to win a prize. If you have won something, then he should simply send it to you with no charge.

When you receive a call from a telemarketer, read through the signs and determine if any of them can be applied to the approach the caller is using. If the answer is yes, you have one of three options:

① Tell the caller to take you off of his or her calling list and hang up the telephone immediately.

② Tell the phone frauder that someone is at the door, then set the telephone on your counter. Hang up the telephone twenty minutes later. If the frauder calls you up again hang up the telephone immediately.

③ Listen to the phone frauder's presentation, ask questions, waste his or her time on the telephone. Get all the information you can about the company, address, telephone numbers, and caller's name. At the end of the pitch, when you are being pressured, tell the phone frauder that it is not nice to lie to people and to take you off his or her calling list.

Option three is the most effective at costing the phone frauder time and money. Use this option only if you feel you have been educated enough to know what you are dealing with over the telephone. The phone frauders are ingenious. You must remember they are lying to you. They think you are gullible. They think you are stupid.

If you have any qualms about using option two, remember, these phone frauders have no respect for you or the truth. They deserve whatever you can give them. It is important to demand that the caller take your name off of his or her calling list and never call you again. Many states have laws which require telemarketers to remove your name from their lists if you request that they do so.

If you know you are easily intimidated and are a current victim of these telephone scams the first thing you need to do is stop. It's that simple. Here are the exact things for you to do and the order in which to do them:

① Change your telephone to an unlisted number right away. Get your last telephone bill, call the number for residential telephone service and change your telephone number. Then call all your friends and neighbors with the new telephone number. Do not put this number on any mail-in entry or survey form.

② If a telephone solicitor calls, hang up the telephone immediately.

③ Brush up on your strategies for becoming an American fraud fighter.

Personal Fraud Fighter Stories

You may have been defrauded once, twice, or twenty times. You may think you have not been defrauded but you were—the frauder may have been so good you didn't know you were scammed. You probably know many people who have been victims of theft and larceny only they haven't told you about what happened. Don Carmichael, a seventy-two-year-old victim from Palmdale, California, told me that he was afraid to report the crimes when he had been the victim of fraud. He was afraid that he would be looked at as if he were losing his mind, not able to control his finances. He owned his own home and was afraid that his family might want him to move to a rest home. He was afraid he would lose control over his life. Once I showed him how to set up his finances, so they were secure from scam artists, his children, and himself, he felt much more in control of his life. There are a percentage of people who cannot seem to say no when pressured or manipulated by a frauder or even a legitimate salesperson.

Over the years John and I have seen many people, especially seniors, take matters in their own hands. What they have done is often not nice and is not legal. We do not suggest you copy them. However, it is nice to see seniors being creative.

Max Welby, an eighty-year-old retired rancher from Wyoming, enjoys packaging steer manure and mailing it to everyone who calls trying to sell him something. He feels most of them are frauders and since he can't tell who was who, he "mails the B.S. to the B.S.'ers." He seals the manure airtight, so it wouldn't smell until the box is opened. Max calls it this his "bouquet box."

Ann Donahue, a sixty-two-year-old lady from Chicago, has a brass whistle her nephew gave her. She ties it to the telephone in the living room. Ann lets the phone frauder finish his or her presentation (pitch) and then she says, "Can I ask you a question?" The frauder always says yes. She waits a couple of seconds, then blows the whistle into the telephone with all her might. She then hangs up the telephone, walks to the front of her mobile home and yells, "I got another one!" Ann only answers her telephone using the speaker phone, in case a frauder wants to call her back to even the score.

There are also seniors who use legal ways to aggravate the frauders.

Harold Jacobson, a sixty-seven-year-old fraud fighter from Miami, likes to tell frauders that he is having problems with his hearing aid. Every few minutes he tells the frauder that the hearing aid stopped working, to hang on while he fixes it. Each time he puts the telephone down for a few minutes, comes back and tells the frauder it's working again. Harold makes the frauders repeat parts of their pitches many times over, wasting their time.

Door-to-Door Fraud

Door-to-door scams have some distinct characteristics just like phone scams. The most common door-to-door frauds involve the sales of deceptive Medigap insurance policies, phony magazine subscriptions, collections for charities and roof, driveway, and window repairs. Common in-person frauds involve the bank examiner hoax, the phony detective/police officer scam, and the equity skimming con. Below are some key signs to look for:

D *escribes a job he or she was doing down the street*

O *bserves something wrong with your roof, house, or life*

O *ffers a huge discount to fix your house or sell a product*

R *equires money in advance to buy supplies or get product*

Describes a job he or she was doing down the street

This is a common approach used by fraudulent contractors who want to rip you off. If you hear this from a stranger at your door, turn him or her away.

Observes something wrong with your roof, house, or life

If a stranger knocks on your door and says there is something wrong with your roof or something else about your home, turn him away. If you continue to be concerned, look up the names of licensed and bonded contractors in the yellow pages and ask them to come out and evaluate the situation.

Offers you a huge discount to fix your roof/put on siding

If a stranger at your door says he or she can give you a great deal on the job, you should still get at least two other bids from reputable contractors before hiring anyone. If the door-to-door contractor was the lowest bidder by a wide margin, choose the second lowest bidder. Always be suspicious of "unbelievably low" prices by contractors, or anyone else for that matter.

Requires money in advance before starting the work

This is a big warning sign. Some legitimate contractors will ask for a 25 percent up-front deposit and payments made as work is completed.

Avoid door-to-door roofers who demand 100 percent of the money in advance. You may never see the job completed.

In this day and age it is not a wise idea to open your door to someone you do not know. If you do answer your door to a stranger politely say you're not interested and turn him away. If he persists, tell him you are going to call the police or the attorney general's office.

MaryAnn Stoppard of Coraopolis, Pennsylvania, used the book's advice on stopping door-to-door solicitors. MaryAnn told me that she finally put up the signs we suggested on the front of her porch and this stopped nine out of ten solicitors from knocking on her door.

We suggest you purchase and install two signs on the front door or porch:

You should have a peephole in your front and back doors. You should be able to see through this hole so you can identify who is at your door. Many people have the old-style small peephole that they cannot see through. The purpose of the peephole is for your safety—physical, mental, and financial. There are peepholes you can purchase that are large enough for you to identify the person knocking on your door. If you do not know the person who is at your front door—do not answer the door. If it is important enough, the person will leave you a note or write you a letter.

If someone approaches you when you are in your yard, the gym, the senior's center, outside a store, or any of the various places in-person frauders operate, politely say you're not interested. If the person continues to pitch you, tell the person you don't have any money. Another "out" is to tell the solicitor a friend of yours is in that business (the business the pitch is about) and is taking care of you. If the person still persists ask for his or her city license number or state license number. Or you can simply say, "Leave me alone or I will scream for the police."

The point is, the best way to eliminate being taken is to eliminate being pitched by one of these mesmerizers. These con men and women will lure you into pleasant conversation and then spring to attack you, to sell you one of their fraudulent goods or services or investments.

Mail Fraud

Mail fraud scams are often very similar if not directly related to phone scams. Most fraudulent telemarketers use direct mail solicitations to develop mooch lists which they then use to victimize consumers. Most of these mailers involve some version of the sweepstakes or free prize promotion.

To illustrate how successful these mailers can be, the normal response rate for a direct mail piece is between 1 and 2 percent. For every 1,000 pieces mailed, between ten and twenty people will respond. In 1993 the United States Postal Service decided to try an innovative strategy to warn potential mail fraud victims. They mailed out 200,000 pieces of mail which notified consumers that they had "already won one of four fabulous prizes." (Sound familiar?)

They provided an 800 number for consumers to call, but instead of the consumer reaching a con artist, the caller was given a tape-recorded message from the Postal Service warning him or her against fraud. The interesting fact is that in response to the 200,000 postcards mailed out, 40,000 people called the 800 number. That is an astounding 20 percent response rate, which explains why so many businesses use the free prize promotion. The following are the five common signs of mail fraud:

M **illion-dollar prize money can be yours**

A **miracle cure has been discovered—send $$$**

I **nstant winnings are yours, call the 900 or 800 number**

L **ottery secrets: pay $$$ to find out how to win**

If you receive mail which contains these pitches or anything resembling them, throw it away immediately. If you have been the victim of mail fraud, notify the U.S. postal inspectors now.

Million-dollar prize money can be yours

This is the most common approach used in mail fraud pitches: the idea that you can get something for nothing. If you receive mail claiming that you have won and all you have to do is send in $5.00 to enter, throw it away. Not only will you not win anything, but you will get placed on a telemarketing fraud boiler room's mailing list and will be solicited to give more money.

A miracle cure has been discovered—send $$$

Any solicitation which claims to have discovered some breakthrough cure for a previously incurable illness is probably fraud. When new cures for diseases are discovered, they are normally first announced by accredited universities, research laboratories, or scientific publications. Consult your physician before taking any new medication.

Instant winnings are yours, call the 900 or 800 number

Anytime someone sends you mail and says you can win, no matter what it is, don't believe the person. Even state-run lotteries give participants only a one in 7 million chance of winning. Remember that often you are receiving award notification from telemarketers so that they will call you and try to take more of your money.

Lottery secrets: pay $$$ to find out how to win

Pay $29.95 to find out how to win: Some mail order fraud operations will tell you they have "cracked the code" for the your state's lottery or for the Canadian lottery. All you have to do is send money to find out this valuable secret. Don't believe it. It is just another way to get you to give away your money.

Personal Fraud Fighter Stories

Herb, a seventy-seven-year-old university professor from Whitefish, Montana, prides himself in being an aggressive fraud fighter who abhors the volumes of junk mail he receives each week. Not only does he refuse to open such mail, but he goes a step further and writes "return to sender" on each envelope, in an attempt to have the sender pay additional postage. He also collects some of the junk mail and sends it to the attorney general's office each month "just to let them know the kind of solicitations that pollute my mailbox," says Herb.

Helen, a sixty-five-year-old retired nurse from Milwaukee, has for the past five years cataloged each piece of junk mail she received. She records the sender's name, address, the type of mailer, when it was received, and how much money the firm is asking for. At the end of each year, she writes a year-end report and sends it to the U.S. Postal Service and the attorney general's office so they can track mail fraud activity for her age group.

"At first the agencies didn't know what to think of me," says Helen. "Now they call me at the end of the year if my report is late. They find it really useful," she says.

Whatever method you employ, your main objective is to destroy the frauders law of numbers, or dramatically decrease them. Now, if everyone learned what these mail frauds are, and threw the mailings away, then the frauders would move on to something else because they would get no responses. You can teach them not to target seniors as their victims.

Remember, if you have been victimized by a mail fraud scam, the best thing to do is contact your local attorney general's office and file a written complaint against the firm. You may also want to send a complaint to the U.S. Postal Service office in your area. There are some people who actually believe that every commercial piece of mail that is delivered through the U.S. Postal Service has been somehow examined and approved by the government. Nothing could be farther from the truth. It would be impossible to examine even a representative example of the millions of pieces that are delivered through the mail each day. So when it comes to avoiding mail fraud, you are on your own.

Discover if you have been the victim of mail fraud, using the outline on the next page to see how many times you have been taken. Go through your checkbook and money orders to see if you wrote any for a purchase through the mail. Go through your papers to see what mail offers you have responded to. Write a separate complaint for each suspected case of fraud. Then you take action, for it is only with your help that we can help America. Start this project now.

FRAUD VICTIM INFORMATION FORM

Your name: ———————————————————————————

Address: —————————————————————————————

City, State, Zip: ———————————————————————————

Home telephone: ———————— Work telephone: ——————————

TYPE OF FRAUD:

Telephone: ———————————————————————————————

Mail: ———————————————————————————————————

In-person: ——————————————————————————————

Door-to-door: ————————————————————————————

DATE CONTACTED:

Salesperson's name: —————————————————————————

Company name: ———————————————————————————

Company address: ————————————————————————————

City, state, and zip code: ————————————————————————

Telephone number: ——————————————————————————

800 number: ——————————————————————————————

Describe promotion offered: ————————————————————————

Describe product offered: ——————————————————————————

Date funds exchanged hands: ———————————————————————

Describe guarantees by company that were not fulfilled: ———————————

—————————————————————————————————————

Date called for refund: ——————————————————————————

Date refund request letter mailed: ———————————————————

Results from contacting company for refund: ——————————————

—————————————————————————————————————

The following letter may also be helpful in getting your money back.

To: Customer Service
Name of company
Address
City, state, zip code

Regarding: Fraudulent representation of product/promotion by (enter salesperson's name here)

On (date) I was contacted by a representative of your company (enter salesperson's name) and was given promises that were not kept during that conversation. (Salesperson's name) promised me:

I am dissatisfied with the merchandise you sent me and would like a complete refund. This letter is being mailed certified mail with a return receipt so I have a legal date of your receipt of this request for refund. Please write me with the details I need so I can return the merchandise and receive my money back.

If I do not receive a response within 14 days I will be forced to make complaints to the Alliance Against Telephone Fraud, the Better Business Bureau, your attorney general's office, my attorney general's office, the U.S. postal inspectors, and the FBI.

I hope your company is legitimate and you do honor this money back request. Nowadays, one cannot be too careful. Thank you for your help.

Sincerely,
(Your name, address, and telephone number)

Regarding TV Infomercials

A growing number of companies are selling their products by purchasing half-hour time slots on the cable television networks emerging throughout the United States. They are intended to look like regular programming despite written disclosures by the station or cable company at the beginning and end of each broadcast.

The typical format is for the product spokesperson to introduce the product and then parade endless numbers of consumers before the camera to give testimonials about the product. The more famous the testifier, the stronger the pitch.

This form of advertising is effective for several reasons. First, the infomercial tends to look like regular programming so the message appears more credible than would a thirty-second commercial.

Secondly, since the entire thirty-minute program is a commercial, there is an uninterrupted period of "brainwashing" or, to be more charitable, "selling," which occurs. Unlike normal programming where the "show" is interrupted by commercials, an infomercial is just one relentless pitch designed to sell even the most reluctant consumer.

There are several things to remember when viewing these infomercials:

① Never invest your hard-earned money in an investment, or an investment opportunity guide, being advertised over an infomercial or a commercial. If there were that much money to be made, why would they tell you about it?

② Consult your family physician before purchasing any diet plans or exercise equipment.

③ Research the products in the consumers guides.

④ Do not invest in a business due to a commercial.

⑤ If it sounds too good to be true, it usually is.

INTERVENTION STRATEGIES FOR FRIENDS, RELATIVES, AND CAREGIVERS

The final step in graduating to fraud fighter status is to learn how to apply your skills to protect others from fraud.

This book began with the story of Emma, an elderly woman who lost her life savings to telemarketers in the two years that followed the death of her husband. Emma began to participate in prize promotions out of boredom and loneliness. Within a short time, telemarketers were calling her, flattering her, sending her flowers on her birthday, and stealing her money. Her daughter at one point tried to intervene, but she was unsuccessful because of the abrasive way she went about it. You will also recall the case of Jill Becker and her mother, Mrs. Anderson, who was befriended by a con artist and spent $100,000 before realizing she was swindled by the "love con." Again, loneliness and isolation left her vulnerable. Finally, the book has provided countless examples of how other swindles target and exploit lonely older adults. The transcript in chapter 6 entitled the Silver Investment Pitch documents in detail how the con artist befriends his victim, Rosie, before moving in for the kill.

But just as there are two main reasons why older adults get taken—lack of education and loneliness—there are two general categories of intervention which prevent fraud: education and companionship.

Education

As a newly appointed American fraud fighter, one of your goals should be to take the information you have learned in this book and share it with at least one other person. The sharing can take many forms. You can act out some of the transcripts in chapter 6, or you can loan a copy of this book to the person you are trying to educate about fraud.

One of the best ways to learn a subject is to teach it. If you are someone who enjoys public speaking, you might want to go down to your local senior center and volunteer to teach a program on fraud, using the material in this book as your source.

You might discover as you visit senior centers that questions arise about the subject. Use the questions and answers in chapter 2 as a guide to answering those questions. You can bet that someone will ask at least one of those questions each time you speak.

One benefit of spreading the word about fraud is that some people will come up afterward and tell you about their experiences as victims, or express concern about some people they think might be falling prey to such schemes. It is your response to these inquiries that will dictate how big your fraud fighter "ministry" will become. The more people you reach, the fewer victims there will be, and the more you will help me reach the goal of touching every older American in this country with fraud prevention information.

Companionship

The story of Emma is a textbook example of how loneliness and isolation can endanger your financial stability and attract con artists by the dozens. Part of your role as an American fraud fighter is to identify those older adults in your community who are socially isolated and therefore vulnerable to fraud, and get them involved in community activities.

If you identify a friend or relative who is recently widowed or living alone, make it your business to visit this person regularly and, during those visits, encourage him or her to participate in some form of social interaction in the community—whether it is going to the senior center, joining a bridge club, taking a class, or volunteering for a nonprofit agency.

In addition, try to assess the person's ability to live by him- or herself and be a catalyst for linking the person up to services he or she might need. Almost every community in the United States has an aging network which provides a variety of services to help older adults remain independent as long as possible. Chapter 8 provides the telephone numbers and state agencies on aging that can direct you to local aging networks. You may simply want to look up the number of your local area agency on aging which can direct you to services available in the community.

Finally, intervening in order to help an older friend or relative can be a delicate matter. Emma became very independent and strong-willed when her daughter attempted to intervene. Emma was angry, and withdrew even further, refusing to talk to her daughter for nearly a year. The trick in effective intervention is to allow the person to preserve his or her dignity and independence while eliminating isolation and loneliness. One of the best ways to strike this delicate balance is to show the person how fun it can be to become involved in the community again, to reintegrate into social circles of people his or her own age.

When you think about it, the only thing con artists do is give the victim something to look forward to in life. Your challenge is to help people find things to look forward to without losing their life savings in the process.

Your Personal Fraud Fighter Stories

I would like to know about how many people you are reaching in your community. Every month or so, you may want to send me information about how many people you educated about fraud or how many you were able to visit and get involved in their communities. Remember, to spread the word you don't necessarily have to give a speech or teach a course on fraud. If you simply have a coffee break or dinner conversation about the subject, you are doing your part as an American fraud fighter.

I would also like to hear from you when you identify new scams which may not be in this book. I am the first to admit that there are new scams being devised every day of the week. If you see one, let me know about it. Send you personal fraud fighter stories to:

 Schemes & Scams
Newcastle Publishing Company, Inc.
P.O. Box 7589
Van Nuys, CA 91409

A FINAL NOTE

This book has hopefully served to raise consumers' awareness of the clever and varied approaches used by con artists to swindle seniors out of their hard-earned money. While we have undoubtedly not covered every scheme that has ever been devised, we have covered every one that John and I have encountered since the late 1970s when we began our involvement in this issue.

One point should be clear to anyone who has read *Schemes and Scams* in its entirety: As long as there is trade and commerce, there will be con artists looking for seniors to victimize. The question is not will you be approached by a con artist, but when.

By learning how the common pitches work and identifying the common elements which con artists prey on, such as the sweepstakes mentality, consumers can begin to arm themselves with the tools they need to protect themselves and avoid fraud.

John and I hope that anyone who reads this book and finds it useful will make a commitment to become an American fraud fighter and pass it onto someone else, perhaps an elderly friend who lives alone.

It is our belief that education and intervention can make a difference in helping reduce fraud in the marketplace. Remember, anyone can be a victim of fraud. So the next time the phone rings and a friendly voice on the other end of the line says, "Congratulations! You've just won. . . ." you should just respond by saying, "You know you're having a bad day when you use that pitch on an American fraud fighter," and hang up.

CHAPTER 8

RESOURCES

This chapter might prove to be the most useful portion of this book for you. When I worked for the attorney general's office, at least one-third of all the calls we received were from consumers who simply didn't know who to call with their problems or questions. This chapter is intended as a resource for consumers whose questions/problems fall into one of three categories:

⮕ Consumer complaints
⮕ Questions about aging services in your community
⮕ Self-help services and miscellaneous other organizations

While this chapter does not contain every organization in existence under these three categories, many major U.S. organizations are included. In developing this resource chapter, every attorney general and state agency on aging was contacted, and updated information provided. As a result of these agencies responding quickly and completely, I believe the information in this chapter represents the most current and up-to-date list of consumer organizations available.

As a newly designated American fraud fighter, one of your challenges is to assist others who may be vulnerable to con artists by linking them up with community organizations and services which can keep them busy and help them fight isolation and loneliness. This chapter should be your starting point in locating those services for loved ones and friends.

Any one of these organizations will tell you they are there to be used. So don't be intimidated, as many are, by the idea of calling the state attorney general's office. Tens of thousands of consumers call these offices each month and your tax dollars are paying for the services they provide. Especially when you are intervening on behalf of a loved one or a relative in need, do not hesitate to exert your rights and find the services that are needed.

ATTORNEY GENERAL OFFICES

Throughout this book, I have made reference to the various attorney general offices around the country. It is my personal bias that of all the agencies working in the area of consumer affairs and protection, the state attorney general offices are by far the most effective, both in terms of mediating complaints and prosecuting con artists.

To follow is a list of attorney general offices for each state. In some states, the governor's office is in charge of consumer complaints, in others, the attorney general is in charge, and still other states have city government offices that handle complaints. Notwithstanding these regional differences, the attorney general's office is a good place to start when filing a complaint or inquiring about a firm.

If you call the attorney general's office in your state to inquire about a particular firm's complaint history, don't be surprised if they refuse to tell you how many complaints have been filed against the firm. In many attorney general's offices, the policy is to tell consumers who call if a firm has been sued by the attorney general. Complaints information is typically not volunteered. However, if you are adamant about pursuing such information, you can ask for a public disclosure request form and, if you fill it out, normally that will allow you to see the complaint file.

STATE OF ALABAMA

Office of the Attorney General
State House, 11 S. Union, Montgomery, AL 36130
Telephone: (205) 242-7300

Call and/or Mail Your Complaint to:
Consumer Affairs Division
State House, 11 S. Union, Montgomery, AL 36130
Out of state residents call: (205) 242-7334
State residents call: (800) 392-5658

STATE OF ALASKA
Office of the Attorney General
P.O. Box K, St. Capitol, Juneau, AK 99811
Telephone: (907) 465-3600
Call and/or Mail Your Complaint to:
Fraud Complaint Director
P.O. Box K, St. Capitol, Juneau, AK 99811
Out of state and state residents call: (907) 465-3600

STATE OF ARIZONA
Office of the Attorney General
1275 W. Washington, Phoenix, AZ 85007
Telephone: (602) 542-4266
Call and/or Mail Your Complaint to:
Complaint Intake Center
1275 W. Washington, Phoenix, AZ 85007
Out of state residents call: (602) 542-5763
State residents call: (800) 352-8431

STATE OF ARKANSAS
Office of the Attorney General
200 Tower Building, 323 Center Street, Little Rock, AR 72201
Telephone: (501) 682-2007
Call and/or Mail Your Complaint to:
Fraud Complaint Director
200 Tower Building, 323 Center Street, Little Rock, AR 72201
Out of state and state residents call: (501) 682-2007

STATE OF CALIFORNIA

Office of the Attorney General
1515 K. Street, Suite 511, Sacramento, CA 95814
Telephone: (916) 445-9555
Call and/or Mail Your Complaint to:
Attorney General Public Inquiry Unit
1515 K. Street, Suite 600, Sacramento, CA 95814
Out of state residents call: (916) 322-3360
State residents call: (800) 952-5225

STATE OF COLORADO

Office of the Attorney General
1525 Sherman Street, Denver, CO 80203
Telephone: (303) 620-4500 or (800) 332-2071
Call and/or Mail Your Complaint to:
Consumer Protection Division
1525 Sherman Street, 5th Floor, Denver, CO 80202
Out of state residents call: (303) 866-5230
State residents call: (303) 332-2071

STATE OF CONNECTICUT

Office of the Attorney General
55 Elm Street, Hartford, CT 06106
Telephone: (203) 566-2026
Call and/or Mail Your Complaint to:
Attorney General Office
55 Elm Street, Hartford, CT 06106
Out of state and state residents call: (203) 566-2026

STATE OF DELAWARE
Office of the Attorney General
820 N. French Street, 8th Floor, Wilmington, DE 19801
Telephone: (302) 577-3838
Call and/or Mail Your Complaint to:
Fraud Complaint Director
820 N. French Street, 8th Floor, Wilmington, DE 19801
Out of state and state residents call: (302) 577-3838

STATE OF FLORIDA
Office of the Attorney General
Pl01 State Capitol, Tallahassee, FL 32399
Telephone: (904) 487-1963
Call and/or Mail Your Complaint to:
Consumer Services
Pl01 State Capitol, Tallahassee, FL 32399
Out of state and state residents call: (904) 488-2221

STATE OF GEORGIA
Office of the Attorney General
132 State Capitol, 40 Capitol Square SW, Atlanta, GA 30334
Telephone: (404) 656-4585
Call and/or Mail Your Complaint to:
Government Office of Consumer Affairs
2 Martin Luther King Jr. Drive, E. Tower, Atlanta, GA 30334
Out of state and state residents call: (404) 656-3790

STATE OF HAWAII
Office of the Attorney General
425 Queen Street, Honolulu, HI 96813
Telephone: (808) 586-1282
Call and/or Mail Your Complaint to:
Office of Consumer Protection
828 Fort Street Mall, Honolulu, HI 96813
Out of state and state residents call: (808) 587-3222

STATE OF IDAHO

Office of the Attorney General
State House, Room 119, Boise, ID 83720
Telephone: (208) 334-2400
Call and/or Mail Your Complaint to:
State House, Room 119, Boise, ID 83720
Out of state residents call: (208) 334-2200
State residents call: (800) 432-3545

STATE OF ILLINOIS

Office of the Attorney General
500 S. 2nd Street, Springfield, IL 62706
Telephone: (217) 782-1090
Call and/or Mail Your Complaint to:
Fraud Complaint Director
500 S. 2nd Street, Springfield, IL 62706
Out of state and state residents call: (217) 782-1090

STATE OF INDIANA

Office of the Attorney General
219 State House, Indianapolis, IN 46204
Telephone: (317) 232-6201
Call and/or Mail Your Complaint to:
Fraud Complaint Director
219 State House, Indianapolis, IN 46204
Out of state and state residents call: (317) 232-6201

STATE OF IOWA

Office of the Attorney General
Hoover State Building, 2nd Floor, Des Moines, IA 50319
Telephone: (515) 281-5164
Call and/or Mail Your Complaint to:
Fraud Complaint Director
Hoover State Building, 2nd Floor, Des Moines, IA 50319
Out of state and state residents call: (515) 281-5164

STATE OF KANSAS

Office of the Attorney General
Judicial Center, 2nd Floor, Topeka, KS 66612
Telephone: (913) 296-2215
Call and/or Mail Your Complaint to:
Complaints/Kansas Attorney General
Judicial Center, 2nd Floor, Topeka, KS 66612
Out of state residents call: (913) 296-3751
State residents call: (800) 432-2310

STATE OF KENTUCKY

Office of the Attorney General
116 State Capitol, Frankfort, KY 40601
Telephone: (502) 564-7600
Call and/or Mail Your Complaint to:
Fraud Complaint Director
116 State Capitol, Frankfort, KY 40601
Out of state and state residents call: (502) 564-7600

STATE OF LOUISIANA

Office of the Attorney General
Department of Justice, 2-3-4 Loyola Building, New Orleans, LA 70112
Telephone: (504) 342-7013
Call and/or Mail Your Complaint to:
Chief, Consumer Protection
Department of Justice, P.O. Box 94095, Baton Rouge, LA 70804
Out of state and state residents call: (504) 342-9638

STATE OF MAINE

Office of the Attorney General
State House, Station #6, Augusta, ME 04330
Telephone: (207) 626-8800
Call and/or Mail Your Complaint to:
Fraud Complaint Director
State House, Station #6, Augusta, ME 04330
Out of state and state residents call: (207) 626-8800

STATE OF MARYLAND
Office of the Attorney General
200 St. Paul Place, Baltimore, MD 21202
Telephone: (301) 576-6300
Call and/or Mail Your Complaint to:
Consumer Protection Division
200 St. Paul Place, Baltimore, MD 21202
Out of state and state residents call: (410) 576-6550

STATE OF MASSACHUSETTS
Office of the Attorney General
One Ashburton Place, Boston, MA 02108
Telephone: (617) 727-7750
Call and/or Mail Your Complaint to:
Fraud Complaint Director
One Ashburton Place, Boston, MA 02108
Out of state residents call: (800) 872-0166
State residents call: (800) 882-2003

STATE OF MICHIGAN
Office of the Attorney General
525 W. Ottawa, P.O. Box 30212, Lansing, MI 48909
Telephone: (517) 373-1110
Call and/or Mail Your Complaint to:
Fraud Complaint Director
525 W. Ottawa, P.O. Box 30212, Lansing, MI 48909
Out of state and state residents call: (517) 373-1110

STATE OF MINNESOTA
Office of the Attorney General
102 State Capitol, St. Paul, MN 55155
Telephone: (612) 296-6196
Call and/or Mail Your Complaint to:
Consumer Services

H400 NCL Tower, 445 Minnesota Street, St. Paul, MN 55155
Out of state residents call: (612) 296-3353
State residents call: (800) 657-3787

STATE OF MISSISSIPPI

Office of the Attorney General
P.O. Box 220, Jackson, MS 39205
Telephone: (601) 359-3680
Call and/or Mail Your Complaint to:
Chief—Consumer Protection Division
P.O. Box 22947, Jackson, MS 39225
Out of state and state residents call: (601) 354-6018

STATE OF MISSOURI

Office of the Attorney General, Public Protection Division
Missouri Supreme Court Building, Jefferson City, MO 65102
Telephone: (601) 359-3680
Call and/or Mail Your Complaint to:
Fraud Complaint Director
Office of the Attorney General, Consumer Protection
P.O. Box 899, Jefferson City, MO 65102
Out of state residents call: (800) 729-8668
State residents call: (800) 392-8222

STATE OF MONTANA

Office of the Attorney General
P.O. Box 201401, 215 N. Sanders, Helena, MT 59620
Telephone: (406) 444-2026
Call and/or Mail Your Complaint to:
Consumer Affairs
1424 9th Avenue, Helena, MT 59620
Out of state and state residents call: (406) 444-3553

STATE OF NEBRASKA
Office of the Attorney General
State Capitol, P.O. Box 98920, Lincoln, NE 68509
Telephone: (402) 471-2682
Call and/or Mail Your Complaint to:
Fraud Complaint Director
State Capitol, P.O. Box 98920, Lincoln, NE 68509
Out of state and state residents call: (402) 471-2682

STATE OF NEVADA
Office of the Attorney General
198 S. Carson Street, Carson City, NV 89710
Telephone: (702) 687-4170
Call and/or Mail Your Complaint to:
Consumer Protection
316 Bridger Street, Suite 200, Las Vegas, NV 89102
Out of state and state residents call: (702) 486-3784

STATE OF NEW HAMPSHIRE
Office of the Attorney General
208 State House Annex, 25 Capitol Street, Concord, NH 03301
Telephone: (603) 271-3641
Call and/or Mail Your Complaint to:
Consumer Protection Bureau
25 Capitol Street, Concord, NH 03301
Out of state and state residents call: (603) 271-3641

STATE OF NEW JERSEY
Office of the Attorney General
25 Market Street, Cn300, Trenton, NJ 08625
Telephone: (609) 292-4925
Call and/or Mail Your Complaint to:
D.C.I., Fraud Bureau
25 Market Street, Trenton, NJ 08625-0085
Out of state and state residents call: (609) 984-3836

STATE OF NEW MEXICO

Office of the Attorney General
Bataan Building, Galisto Street, Santa Fe, NM 87504
Telephone: (505) 827-6792
Call and/or Mail Your Complaint to:
Consumer Protection Division
P.O. Drawer 1508, Santa Fe, NM 87504
Out of state residents call: (505) 827-6060
State residents call: (800) 678-1508

STATE OF NEW YORK

Office of the Attorney General
120 Broadway, Floor 3, New York, NY 10271
Telephone: (212) 416-8345
Call and/or Mail Your Complaint to:
State of New York, Department of Law
120 Broadway, Floor 3, New York, NY 10271
Out of state and state residents call: (212) 416-8345

STATE OF NORTH CAROLINA

Office of the Attorney General
Division of Aging
CB 2953, 693 Palmer Drive, Raleigh, NC 27626
Telephone: (919) 733-3983
Call and/or Mail Your Complaint to:
NC Consumer Protection Division
P.O. Box 629, Raleigh, NC 27602
Out of state residents call: (919) 733-7741 or (800) 662-7030
State residents call: (919) 733-7741

STATE OF NORTH DAKOTA

Office of the Attorney General
State Capitol, 600 East Boulevard, Bismarck, ND 58505
Telephone: (701) 224-2210
Call and/or Mail Your Complaint to:
Consumer Protection
State Capitol, 600 East Boulevard, Bismarck, ND 58505
Out of state residents call: (800) 472-2600
State residents call: (701) 224-3404

STATE OF OHIO

Office of the Attorney General
State Office Tower, Floor 17, 30 E. Broad Street, Columbus, OH 43266
Telephone: (614) 466-3376
Call and/or Mail Your Complaint to:
Consumer Protection Section
St. Office Tower, Floor 25, 30 E. Broad Street, Columbus, OH 43266
Out of state residents call: (614) 466-4986
State residents call: (800) 282-0515

STATE OF OKLAHOMA

Office of the Attorney General
State Capitol, Oklahoma City, OK 73105
Telephone: (405) 521-3921
Call and/or Mail Your Complaint to:
Consumer Protection Division
4545 N. Lincoln, Suite 260, Oklahoma City, OK 73105
Out of state residents call: (405) 521-4274
State residents call: (405) 521-2029

STATE OF OREGON

Office of the Attorney General
100 Justice Building, Salem, OR 97310
Telephone: (503) 378-6002

Call and/or Mail Your Complaint to:
Consumer Protection Services
100 Justice Building, Salem, OR 97310
Out of state and state residents call: (503) 378-4320

STATE OF PENNSYLVANIA
Office of the Attorney General
Strawberry Square, 14th Floor, Harrisburg, PA 17120
Telephone: (717) 787-3391
Call and/or Mail Your Complaint To:
Consumer Protection Division
Strawberry Square, 14th Floor, Harrisburg, PA 17120
Out of state residents call: (717) 787-9707
State residents call: (800) 441-2555

STATE OF RHODE ISLAND
Office of the Attorney General
72 Pine Street, Providence, RI 02903
Telephone: (401) 274-4400
Call and/or Mail Your Complaint to:
Fraud Complaint Director
72 Pine Street, Providence, RI 02903
Out of state and state residents call: (401) 274-4400

STATE OF SOUTH CAROLINA
Office of the Attorney General
Robert Dennis Office Building, P.O. Box 11549, Columbia, SC 29211
Telephone: (803) 734-3970
Call and/or Mail Your Complaint to:
Fraud Complaint Director
Robert Dennis Office Building, P.O. Box 11549, Columbia, SC 29211
Out of state residents call: (803) 737-9452
State residents call: (800) 922-1594

STATE OF SOUTH DAKOTA

Office of the Attorney General
State Capitol, 500 E. Capitol, Pierre, SD 57501
Telephone: (605) 773-3215
Call and/or Mail Your Complaint to:
State Capitol, 500 E. Capitol, Pierre, SD 57501
Out of state residents call: (605) 773-4400
State residents call: (800) 300-1986

STATE OF TENNESSEE

Office of the Attorney General
450 Robertson Parkway, Nashville, TN 37423
Telephone: (615) 741-3491
Call and/or Mail Your Complaint to:
Division of Consumer Affairs
500 James Robertson Parkway, Nashville, TN 37219
Out of state and state residents call: (615) 741-3491

STATE OF TEXAS

Office of the Attorney General
Capitol Station, P.O. Box 12548, Austin, TX 78711
Telephone: (512) 463-2100
Call and/or Mail Your Complaint to:
Consumer Protection
Capitol Station, P.O. Box 12548, Austin, TX 8711
Out of state residents call: (512) 463-2100
State residents call: (800) 621-0508

STATE OF UTAH

Office of the Attorney General
236 State Capitol, Salt Lake City, UT 84114
Telephone: (801) 538-1015
Call and/or Mail Your Complaint to:
Division of Consumer Rights

236 State Capitol, Salt Lake City, UT 84114
Out of state and state residents call: (801) 538-1331

STATE OF VERMONT

Office of the Attorney General
Pavilion Office Building, 109 State Street, Montpelier, VT 05609
Telephone: (802) 828-3171
Call and/or Mail Your Complaint to:
Consumer Assistance Program
Uvm, 104 Morrill Hall, Burlington, VT 05401
Out of state residents call: (802) 656-3183
State residents call: (800) 649-2424

STATE OF VIRGINIA

Office of the Attorney General
101 N. 8th Street, 5th Floor, Richmond, VA 23219
Telephone: (804) 786-2071
Call and/or Mail Your Complaint to:
Fraud Complaint Director
101 N. 8th Street, 5th Floor, Richmond, VA 23219
Out of state and state residents call: (804) 786-2071

STATE OF WASHINGTON

Office of the Attorney General
P.O. Box 40100, Olympia, WA 98504
Telephone: (206) 753-6200
Call and/or Mail Your Complaint to:
Consumer Protection Bureau
P.O. Box 40100, Olympia, WA 98504
Out of state residents call: (206) 753-6200
State residents call: (800) 276-9883

STATE OF WEST VIRGINIA

Office of the Attorney General

State Capitol, Room 26-E, Charleston, WV 25305

Telephone: (304) 348-2021

Call and/or Mail Your Complaint to:

Antitrust and Consumer Protection Division

812 Quarrier Street, Floor 16, Charleston, WV 25301

Out of state residents call: (304) 558-8986

State residents call: (800) 368-8808

STATE OF WISCONSIN

Office of the Attorney General

114 East State Capitol, P.O. Box 7857, Madison, WI 53707

Telephone: (608) 266-1221

Call and/or Mail Your Complaint to:

Wisconsin Attorney General of Consumer Protection

114 East State Capitol, P.O. Box 7857, Madison, WI 53707

Out of state residents call: (608) 266-1852

State residents call: (800) 362-8189

STATE OF WYOMING

Office of the Attorney General

123 State Capitol, Cheyenne, WY 82002

Telephone: (307) 777-7841

Call and/or Mail Your Complaint to:

Consumer Protection Division

123 State Capitol, Cheyenne, WY 82002

Out of state and in state residents call: (307) 777-7874

STATE AGENCIES ON AGING

The information to follow provides you with the address and phone number for the state agency on aging for each state. These offices can help direct you to the area agencies on aging in your community, and other services which might be available such as chore service programs, companionship programs, information, referral numbers, and general assistance. The source of this information is the *Consumer's Resource Handbook*, 1992 Edition, Government Printing Office. Published by the United States Office of Consumer Affairs.

ALABAMA COMMISSION ON AGING
136 Catoma Street, Montgomery, AL 36130
(205) 242-5743   (800) 243-5463

ALASKA OLDER ALASKANS COMMISSION
P.O. Box C, Juneau, AK 99811-0209
(907) 465-3250

ARIZONA DEPARTMENT OF ECONOMIC SECURITY
1789 W. Jefferson, 950A, Phoenix, AZ 85007
(602) 542-4446

ARKANSAS OFFICE OF AGING AND ADULT SERVICES
P.O. Box 1437, Little Rock, AR 72203-1437
(501) 682-2441   (800) 482-8049

CALIFORNIA DEPARTMENT OF AGING
1600 K. Street, Sacramento, CA 95814
(916) 322-5290   (800) 231-4024

COLORADO DEPARTMENT OF SOCIAL SERVICES
1575 Sherman Street, Denver, CO 80203-1714
(303) 866-5700

CONNECTICUT DEPARTMENT OF SOCIAL SERVICES
Elderly Services Division
175 Main Street, Hartford, CT 06106
(203) 566-3238   (800) 443-9946

DISTRICT OF COLUMBIA OFFICE OF AGING
1424 K. Street, NW, 2nd Floor, Washington, DC 20005
(202) 724-5622

DELAWARE HEALTH AND SOCIAL SERVICES
Division of Aging
1901 N. Dupont Highway, New Castle, DE 19720
(302) 577-4791   (800) 223-9074

FLORIDA DEPARTMENT OF ELDER AFFAIRS
1317 Winewood Boulevard, Building 1, Room 317
Tallahassee, FL 32399-0700
(904) 922-5297

GEORGIA DEPARTMENT OF HUMAN SERVICES
2 Peachtree Street, Suite 18-310, Atlanta, GA 30303
(404) 894-5333

HAWAII EXECUTIVE OFFICE ON AGING
Office of the Governor
335 Merchant Street, Room 241, Honolulu, HI 96813
(808) 586-0100   (800) 468-4644

IDAHO OFFICE ON AGING
Statehouse, Room 108, Boise, ID 83720
(208) 334-3833

STATE OF ILLINOIS DEPARTMENT ON AGING
421 E. Capitol Avenue, Springfield, IL 62701
(217) 785-2870   (800) 252-8966

INDIANA AGING SERVICES DIVISION
P.O. Box 7083, Indianapolis, IN 46207-7083
(317) 232-7020   (800) 622-4972

IOWA DEPARTMENT OF ELDER AFFAIRS
914 Grand Avenue, Suite 236, Des Moines, IA 50319
(515) 281-5187   (800) 532-3213

KANSAS DEPARTMENT ON AGING
915 SW Harrison Street, Room 122S, Topeka, KS 66612-1500
(913) 296-4986   (800) 432-3535

KENTUCKY DEPARTMENT OF SOCIAL SERVICES
Division of Aging
Cabinet for Human Resource
275 E. Main Street, 5th Floor W., Frankfort, KY 40621
(502) 564-6930   (800) 372-2991

LOUISIANA OFFICE OF THE GOVERNOR
Office of Elderly Affairs
P.O. Box 80374, Baton Rouge, LA 70898
(504) 925-1700

MAINE BUREAU OF ELDER AND ADULT SERVICES
35 Anthony Avenue, Station 11, Augusta, ME 04333-0011
(207) 626-5335

MARYLAND OFFICE ON AGING
301 W. Preston, Floor 10, Baltimore, MD 21201
(301) 225-1100   (800) 243-3425

MASSACHUSETTS EXECUTIVE OFFICES OF ELDER AFFAIRS
38 Chauncy Street, Boston, MA 02111
(617) 727-7750   (800) 882-2003

MICHIGAN SERVICES TO THE AGING

P.O. Box 30026, Lansing, MI 48909
(517) 373-8230

MINNESOTA BOARD ON AGING

444 Lafayette Road, St. Paul, MN 55155-3843
(612) 296-2544   (800) 333-2433

MISSISSIPPI DIVISION OF AGING AND ADULT SERVICES

421 W. Pascagoula Street, Jackson, MS 39203
(601) 949-2070   (800) 345-6347

MISSOURI DIVISION OF AGING

P.O. Box 1337, Jefferson City, MO 65102
(314) 751-8535   (800) 392-0210

MONTANA AGING SERVICES

Governor's Office
Helena, MT 59620
(406) 444-4204   (800) 253-4093

NEBRASKA DEPARTMENT ON AGING

P.O. Box 95044, Lincoln, NE 68509
(402) 471-2306

STATE OF NEVADA DIVISION FOR AGING SERVICE

340 N. 11th Street, Suite 114, Las Vegas, NV 89101
(702) 486-3545   (800) 243-3638

NEW HAMPSHIRE DIVISION OF ELDERLY AND ADULT SERVICES

115 Pleasant Street, Annex Building #1, Concord, NH 03301-3843
(603) 271-4390   (800) 351-1888

STATE OF NEW JERSEY DEPARTMENT OF COMMUNITY AFFAIRS

Division On Aging

101 S. Broad Street, Cn 807, Trenton, NJ 08625
(609) 292-3766   (800) 792-8820

NEW MEXICO STATE AGENCY ON AGING
224 E. Palace Avenue, 4th Floor, Santa Fe, NM 87501
(505) 827-7640   (800) 432-2080

NEW YORK OFFICE FOR THE AGING
Agency Building 2, ESP
Albany, NY 12223
(518) 474-5731   (800) 342-9871

NORTH CAROLINA DIVISION OF AGING
Caller Box 2953, 693 Palmer Drive, Raleigh, NC 27626-0531
(919) 733-3983   (800) 662-7030

NORTH DAKOTA AGING SERVICES
600 East Boulevard, Bismarck, ND 58505
(701) 224-2310   (800) 755-8921

OHIO DEPARTMENT OF AGING
50 W. Broad Street, 8th Floor, Columbus, OH 43266-0501
(614) 466-5500   (800) 282-1206

OKLAHOMA
Special Unit On Aging
P.O. Box 25352, Oklahoma City, OK 73125
(405) 521-2281

OREGON DHR, SENIOR AND DISABLED SERVICES DIVISION
500 Summer Street NE, 2nd Floor, Salem, OR 97310
(503) 378-4728   (800) 286-8096

COMMONWEALTH OF PENNSYLVANIA
DEPARTMENT OF AGING
400 Market Street, State Office Building, Harrisburg, PA 17101
(717) 783-1550

STATE OF RHODE ISLAND
DEPARTMENT OF ELDERLY AFFAIRS
160 Pine Street, Providence, RI 02903
(401) 277-2880   (800) 322-2880

SOUTH CAROLINA GOVERNOR'S OFFICE
Division On Aging
400 Arbor Lake Drive, Suite 301, Columbia, SC 29223
(803) 735-0210   (800) 868-9095

SOUTH DAKOTA OFFICE OF ADULT SERVICES AND AGING
700 Governors Drive, Pierre, SD 57501
(605) 773-3656

TENNESSEE COMMISSION ON AGING
706 Church Street, Suite 201, Nashville, TN 37243-0860
(615) 741-2056   (800) 848-0249

TEXAS DEPARTMENT ON AGING
P.O. Box 12786, Capitol Station, Austin, TX 78711
(512) 444-2727   (800) 252-9240

UTAH DEPARTMENT OF HUMAN SERVICES
Division of Aging and Adult Services
P.O. Box 45500, Salt Lake City, UT 84145-0500
(801) 530-7631

VERMONT DEPARTMENT OF AGING AND DISABLED
103 S. Main Street, Waterbury, VT 05671-2301
(802) 241-2400

VIRGINIA DEPARTMENT FOR THE AGING
700 E. Franklin Street, 10th Floor, Richmond, VA 23219
(804) 225-2271   (800) 552-4464

WASHINGTON AGING AND ADULT SERVICES ADMINISTRATION
Ob-44a, Olympia, WA 98504
(206) 493-2509   (800) 422-3263

WEST VIRGINIA COMMISSION ON AGING
State Capitol, Charleston, WV 25305
(304) 348-3317

WISCONSIN BUREAU ON AGING
P.O. Box 7851, Madison, WI 53707
(608) 266-2536

STATE OF WYOMING DEPARTMENT OF HEALTH
139 Hathaway Building, Cheyenne, WY 82002-0480
(307) 777-7986   (800) 442-2766

FEDERAL AGENCIES

A majority of the time, it is more effective to contact state or local consumer agencies than the federal government. The primary role of federal agencies is to focus on large, investigative issues that affect huge numbers of consumers. The agencies listed here should be viewed this way, and are provided in the event you become aware of a major fraud scheme which is operating in multiple states. The source of this information is the *Consumer's Resource Handbook*, 1992 Edition, Government Printing Office. Published by the United States Office of Consumer Affairs.

FEDERAL BUREAU OF INVESTIGATION

There are many regional offices throughout the United States. Look inside the front cover of your telephone directory for the number of the nearest FBI regional office. If the number does not appear there look under "U.S. Government, Federal Bureau of Investigation." You may also wish to contact:

FBI
Department of Justice
Washington, DC 20535
(202) 324-3000

U.S. POSTAL DEPARTMENT

Contact your local postal inspector. Look in your telephone directory under "U.S. Government Postal Service" for the local listing. If you do not find one near you contact:

Chief Postal Inspector
United States Postal Service
Washington, DC 20260-2100
(202) 268-4267

SECURITIES AND EXCHANGE COMMISSION

The Securities and Exchange Commission is a federal agency which oversees registration of investment firms that offer certain kinds of investments to the public.

Securities and Exchange Commission
Office of Filings, Information and Consumer Services
450 5th Street, NW (Mail Stop 2-6)
Washington, DC 20549
For Investor Complaints:
(202) 272-7440

SELF-HELP GROUPS AND CLEARINGHOUSES

When people feel overwhelmed by personal problems they are at a much higher risk of becoming victimized by telephone fraud. Con artists especially like to take advantage of people who are lonely and depressed. Self-help groups have proven to be a viable way for people to overcome problems in their lives, as well as a means of establishing a social network. The explosive growth of self-help groups has been the result of their success.

There are many self-help groups listed in this chapter; some are national, others are local. They cover an array of topics. You'll notice that some of the entries do not contain addresses. This is because these are "hotlines," the numbers of which connect you to a recorded message or prompt you to input information.

Self-help clearinghouses refer individuals to self-help groups in their area. The telephones are normally handled by volunteers, who have computer access to support group information. Group names, addresses, explanations, telephone numbers, and meeting days and times are provided to the caller. Self-help groups are either free or available at a minimal cost ($5 to $10 a meeting). Nationwide there are groups for over 250 different types of problems.

Look on the following page for your state of residence. If your state does not have a self-help clearinghouse call the national numbers.

CA	(800) 222-5465	**NJ**	(800) 367-6274
CO	(302) 221-9165	**NY**	(718) 596-6000 *(Manhattan)*
CT	(203) 789-7645	**NY**	(518) 474-6293
DC	(703) 536-4100	**NY**	(516) 348-3030 *(Long Island)*
IA	(800) 383-4777	**NY**	(914) 347-3620 *(Westchester)*
IL	(800) 322-6274	**OH**	(513) 225-3004
KS	(800) 445-0116	**OR**	(503) 222-5555
MA	(413) 545-2313	**PA**	(412) 261-5363 *(Pittsburgh)*
MI	(800) 752-5858	**PA**	(717) 961-1234
MI	(517) 484-7373	**RI**	(401) 277-2231
MN	(612) 224-1133	**SC**	(803) 791-9227
MO	(816) 561-4357	**TN**	(615) 584-6736
MO	(314) 773-1399	**TX**	(512) 454-3706
NC	(704) 331-9500	**VA**	(703) 536-4100
NE	(402) 476-9688		

You can also receive self-help information by writing to:

The American Self-Help
Clearinghouse
25 Pocono Road
Denville, NJ 07834
(201) 625-9565

The National Self-Help
Clearinghouse
25 West 43rd Street
Denville, NJ 07834
(201) 625-9053

AGING IN AMERICA
1500 Pelham Parkway, Bronx, NY 10461
(800) 845-6900
A full-service senior center including meals, programs of activity, including dance, art, woodwork, music, and exercise.

ALLIANCE OF GENETIC SUPPORT GROUPS
35 Wisconsin Circle, Suite 440, Chevy Chase, MD 20815
(800) 336-4363
Provides referral and information services on genetic disorders, as well as technical assistance to support groups.

ALZHEIMER'S DISEASE ASSOCIATION, NATIONAL HEADQUARTERS
919 N. Michigan Avenue, Suite 1000, Chicago, IL 60611
(800) 272-3900
Provides literature, and referrals to local chapters. Phone number also functions as a hotline.

AMERICAN ASSOCIATION OF RETIRED PERSONS
601 E Street, NW, Washington, DC 20036
(800) 424-3410
Provides a variety of programs and services for its 35 million members throughout the U.S. It is the largest retirement organization in the U.S.

B'NAI B'RITH WOMEN
1828 L Street, NW, Suite 250, Washington, DC 20036
(202) 857-1300
Jewish women's organization. Interests include emotional health of children and youth; family issues such as choice, domestic violence, long-term health care, civil and constitutional rights, anti-semitism, and community services.

CENTER FOR WOMEN'S POLICY STUDIES
2000 P Street, NW, Washington, DC 20036

(202) 872-1770

A policy advocacy organization concerned with educational and employment equity for women, women and AIDS, violence against women, economic opportunity for low-income women, and reproductive laws.

CHURCH WOMEN UNITED

110 Maryland Avenue, NE, Washington, DC 20002

(202) 544-8747

Christian women's organization. Interests include defense policy, employment, family stability, health, human rights, justice, world peace, hunger and poverty issues, especially as they affect women and children.

COMMUNITY ADDICTIONS PROGRAM

1402 State Boulevard, Fort Wayne, IN 46805

(800) 932-4213

An addiction group therapy program, from court referrals.

CONSUMER FEDERATION OF AMERICA

1424 16th Street, NW, Suite 604, Washington, DC 20036

(202) 387-6121

A federation of national, regional, state, and local pro-consumer organizations. Promotes consumer interests in banking, credit, and insurance; telecommunications; housing; food, drug, and medical care; safety; and natural resources development.

CONSUMER INFORMATION ORDER LINE

(719) 948-4000

Obtain a free consumer information catalog by calling this number.

CONSUMER PRODUCT SAFETY COMMISSION HOTLINE

(800) 638-2772

Provides product recall and safety information on consumer products used around the home and for consumer purposes; provides product safety updates and tips; consumers can report a hazardous product or product-related injury on this line.

CONSUMER UNION OF THE UNITED STATES

1666 Connecticut Avenue, NW, Suite 310, Washington, DC 20009

(202) 462-6262

A consumer advocacy group whose Washington office represents consumer interests before Congress and regulatory agencies; litigates consumer affairs cases involving the government. The main office tests, rates, and reports on competing brands of automobiles, appliances, etc.

DEPARTMENT OF COMMERCE

Office of Consumer Affairs

14th and Constitution Avenue, NW, Room 5718, Washington, DC 20230

(202) 482-2000, ext. 5001

Although they do not enforce any consumer protection laws, this office will mediate consumer complaints with businesses to reach mutually agreeable solutions.

THE ELDERCARE LOCATOR HOTLINE

(800) 677-1116

Offers adult day care, home health, legal services, various senior services.

ELDER CARE PLAN

1701 NE 164th Street, North Miami Beach, FL 33162

(800) 643-5337

Provides home health care services.

ELDER CARE SOLUTIONS

1220 Bardstown Road, Louisville, KY 40204

(800) 633-5723

Provides a host of services, including in-home health care, non-medical care, sitters and companions.

ETHICS AND CONSUMER AFFAIRS OFFICE

1101 17th Street, NW, Suite 705, Washington, DC 20019

(202) 347-1222

Membership is made up of telemarketers, users, creators, and producers of direct mail and suppliers to industry. Conducts research and promotes knowledge and use of direct response marketing. Handles consumer complaints about phone and mail order purchases.

LIFEPLANS

Family Caring Network
2 University Office Park, 51 Sawyer Road, Suite 340
Walthan, MA 02154
(800) 525-7279

Works with insurance agencies who sell long-term care insurance and those who have long-term care as part of their insurance program; they have a program that they developed with B'Nai B'rith called "The Caring Connection," an information and referral assistance program that helps the older adult or his or her family members with aging issues and adult day health care. Provides resources for the elderly, referrals to community services, and information on diseases that affect older adults. A centralized way to get information and help either over the phone or in person.

FAMILY INFORMATION SERVICES

7800 River Road, North Bergen, NJ 07047
(800) 526-9038

A publishing company that provides drug prevention materials to police departments and community alliance programs, such as "Neighborhood Watch" programs.

FEDERAL COMMUNICATIONS COMMISSION

Office of Small Business Activities
119 23rd Street, NW, Washington, DC 20554
(202) 632-1571

This office is the national advocate for small, minority, and female business issues in the telecommunications industry. Provides technical and legal guidance and assistance to the small, minority, and female business community. Serves as the official liaison between federal agencies, state and local governments, and trade associations representing small, minority, and female enterprises concerning FCC policies, procedures, and rule-making activities.

GENERAL FEDERATION OF WOMEN'S CLUB

1734 N Street NW, Washington, DC 20036
(202) 347-3168
Nondenominational, nonpartisan international organization of women volunteers. Interests include conservation, education, home life, international affairs, public affairs, and the arts.

GRIEF RECOVERY HOTLINE

Grief Recovery Center
8306 Wilshire Boulevard, Suite 21A, Beverly Hills, CA 90211
(800) 445-4808
Provides counseling for grievers, and refers callers to 1,200 recovery outreach programs throughout the United States.

HELP AT HOME

P.O. Box 1337, Grenada, MS 38901
(800) 446-4719
Sells and rents durable medical equipment for home health care; helps determine the level of assistance an older adult needs at home.

ACCESSCARE, INC.

2203 North Lois Avenue, Suite 1150, Tampa, FL 33607
(800) 458-6139
Provides managmental and behavioral health care. Helps older adults access mental health benefits from their insurance agencies.

NATIONAL ASSOCIATION OF AREA AGENCIES ON AGING

1112 16th Street, NW, Suite 100, Washington, DC 20036
(800) 677-1116
Provides information and referrals about services and agencies around the country that can help older adults.

NATIONAL ASSOCIATION OF CONSUMER AGENCY ADMINISTRATION

1010 Vermont Avenue, NW, Suite 514, Washington, DC 20005

(202) 347-7395

Seeks to enhance consumer services available to the public. Acts as a clearinghouse for consumer information and legislation. Serves as a liaison with federal agencies and Congress.

NATIONAL ASSOCIATION OF REHABILITATION FACILITIES

P.O. Box 17675, Washington, DC 20041

(800) 368-3513

Works with health care providers and provides education, seminars, research, and referrals and works with Congress on behalf of laws for the disabled.

NATIONAL CONSUMERS LEAGUE

815 15th Street, NW, Suite 928-N, Washington, DC 20005

(202) 639-8140

A citizens' interest group that engages in research and education activities related to consumer issues. Interests include health care; food, drug, and product safety; and telecommunications. Provides financial services.

NATIONAL COUNCIL ON ALCOHOLISM AND DRUG DEPENDENCE HOPE LINE

(800) 622-2255

Call, input your zip code, and they will refer you to an affiliated program and phone number nearest you.

NATIONAL INSURANCE CONSUMER HELPLINE

(800) 942-4242

Provides brochures for Medicare supplement plans.

NATIONAL LITERACY HOTLINE

P.O. Box 81826, Lincoln, NE 68501

(800) 228-8813

Provides extensive information and referrals. They publish a newsletter containing information related to literacy, which can be obtained by writing to the above address.

NATIONAL LIVING WILL REGISTRY

775-NE 79th Street, Suite A, Miami, FL 33138

(800) 222-6597

FAX them living will documents and medical information from living wills for consultation.

NATIONAL ORGANIZATION FOR RARE DISORDERS

P.O. Box 8923, 100R37, New Fairfield, CT 06812

(800) 999-6673

A clearinghouse for information on rare disorders.

NATIONAL PARKINSON FOUNDATION

1501 NW 9th Avenue, Miami, FL 33136

(800) 327-4545

Provides clinical and therapeutic services, public education, and grants.

NATIONAL WOMEN'S LAW CENTER

1616 P Street NW, Washington, DC 20036

(202) 328-5160

Works to expand and protect women's legal rights through litigation, advocacy, and public information. Interests include child care, reproductive rights, education, employment, and women in prison.

ODPHP NATIONAL HEALTH INFORMATION

P.O. Box 1133, Washington, DC 20012

(800) 336-4797

National referrals on health issues specifically on disease and health promotion.

OLDER WOMEN'S LEAGUE

730 11th Street, NW, Suite 300, Washington, DC 20001

(202) 783-6686

A grass roots membership organization concerned with social and economic problems with middle-age/older women. Areas of interest include health care, social security, pension rights, housing, employment, women as caregivers, effects of budget cuts.

SENIOR VENTURES

Central Washington University
Ellensburg, WA 98926
(800) 752-4380
Similar to Elderhostel, this organization is designed for active retired adults. Includes classes and recreational activities.

SMALL BUSINESS ADMINISTRATION

Office of Consumer Affairs
(800) U-ASK-SBA
Answers questions relating to small business and consumer issues.

SUPPORT SERVICES ALLIANCE

P.O. Box 130, 102 Prospect Street, Schoharie, NY 12157
(800) 322-3920
Offers programs and services to the small businessperson and the self-employed.

U.S. OFFICE OF CONSUMER AFFAIRS

Health and Human Services
1620 L Street, NW, Suite 700, Washington, DC 20036
(202) 634-9610
Works on consumer issues with Congress, testifies on consumer issues, such as privacy and fraud, and publishes the Consumer's Resource Handbook, *a guide to all state and local consumer agencies, and attorney general offices. The goal of the handbook is to educate the consumer on the appropriate congressional offices to send complaints. To obtain a free copy, write: Handbook, Consumer Information Center, Pueblo, CO 81009.*

VOLUNTEER EXPRESS

P.O. Box 100886, Nashville, TN 37224-0886
(800) 251-1015
Helps to connect older adults with volunteer services.

THE WOMAN ACTIVIST FUND

(703) 573-8716

An advocacy group that conducts research on individuals and groups in elective and appointed offices, especially as they affect women and minorities. Publishes an annual rating of these officials.

WOMEN'S HEALTHCARE CONSULTANTS

500 Davis Street, Suite 700, Evanston, IL 60201

(800) 543-3854

Publish two newsletters, Regarding Women and Health Care *and* Healthy Decisions, *which specifically address health care issues and their effect on women. Also can refer consumers on a variety of health-related topics.*

WOMEN'S RESEARCH AND EDUCATION INSTITUTION

1700 18th Street, NW, Suite 400, Washington, DC 20009

(202) 328-7070

Provides data, research, policy analyses of women's issues. Sponsors fellowships in congressional offices, promotes public education through conferences, symposia, and briefings, and serves as an information clearinghouse.

ABOUT THE AUTHORS

Doug **Shadel** is one of the most knowledgeable experts in America on the subject of fraud that targets older people. Shadel was a fraud investigator for ten years with the Washington State Attorney General's office, during which time he worked on hundreds of investigations involving seniors. He spent four years as a special assistant to the attorney general, where he directed statewide fraud prevention efforts, gave hundreds of speeches, and wrote numerous brochures and newsletters about fraud. In fact, over 1 million copies of Shadel's brochures have been printed and distributed throughout the United States. The Stop Fraud Network, a fraud prevention program for seniors which Shadel created, was voted outstanding consumer education program in the United States in 1991. Currently, Shadel is an economic security/consumer representative for the American Association of Retired Persons (AARP).

John **T.** is an expert on schemes and scams, having spent ten years as one of the most notorious con artists in telemarketing fraud. John T. not only worked in fraud boiler rooms but for a period of time traveled around the country training new phone fraud con artists how to rip consumers off. Telephone sales pitches he and others developed in the early days of phone fraud trade are still in use today and are among the most effective pitches used to target seniors. For the past three years John T. has been working as a consultant to the Washington State Crime Prevention Association and the Washington State Attorney General's office.

Together, Shadel and John T. have developed some of the best fraud prevention videos, brochures, newsletters, and prevention strategies available to consumers. Now they have produced a comprehensive inside look at virtually every type of fraud scheme in existence today.